Pentaho Analytics for MongoDB Cookbook

Over 50 recipes to learn how to use Pentaho Analytics and MongoDB to create powerful analysis and reporting solutions

Joel Latino

Harris Ward

[PACKT] PUBLISHING

open source
community experience distilled

BIRMINGHAM - MUMBAI

Pentaho Analytics for MongoDB Cookbook

First published: December 2015

Production reference: 1181215

Published by Packt Publishing Ltd.
Livery Place
35 Livery Street
Birmingham B3 2PB, UK.

ISBN 978-1-78355-327-3

www.packtpub.com

Credits

Authors
Joel Latino

Harris Ward

Reviewers
Rio Bastian

Mark Kromer

Commissioning Editor
Usha Iyer

Acquisition Editor
Nikhil Karkal

Content Development Editor
Anish Dhurat

Technical Editor
Menza Mathew

Copy Editor
Vikrant Phadke

Project Coordinator
Bijal Patel

Proofreader
Safis Editing

Indexer
Rekha Nair

Production Coordinator
Manu Joseph

Cover Work
Manu Joseph

About the Authors

Joel Latino was born in Ponte de Lima, Portugal, in 1989. He has been working in the IT industry since 2010, mostly as a software developer and BI developer.

He started his career at a Portuguese company and specialized in strategic planning, consulting, implementation, and maintenance of enterprise software that is fully adapted to its customers' needs.

He earned his graduate degree in informatics engineering from the School of Technology and Management of Viana do Castelo Polytechnic Institute.

In 2014, he moved to Edinburgh, Scotland, to work for Ivy Information Systems, a highly specialized open source BI company in the United Kingdom.

Joel mainly focuses on open source web technology, databases, and business intelligence, and is fascinated by mobile technologies. He is responsible for developing some plugins for Pentaho, such as Android and Apple push notification steps, and lot of other plugins under Ivy Information Systems.

> I would like to thank my family for supporting me throughout my career and endeavors.

Harris Ward has been working in the IT sector since 2004, initially developing websites using LAMP and moving on to business intelligence in 2006. His first role was based in Germany on a product called InfoZoom, where he was introduced to the world of business intelligence. He later discovered open source business intelligence tools and dedicated the last 9 years to not only working on developing solutions, but also working to expand the Pentaho community with the help of other committed members.

Harris has worked as a Pentaho consultant over the past 7 years under Ambient BI. Later, he decided to form Ivy Information Systems Scotland, a company focused on delivering more advanced Pentaho solutions as well as developing a wide range of Pentaho plugins that you can find in the marketplace today.

About the Reviewers

Rio Bastian is a happy software engineer. He has worked on various IT projects. He is interested in business intelligence, data integration, web services (using WSO2 API or ESB), and tuning SQL and Java code. He has also been a Pentaho business intelligence trainer for several companies in Indonesia and Malaysia. Currently, Rio is working on developing one of Garuda Indonesia airline's e-commerce channel web service systems in PT. Aero Systems Indonesia.

In his spare time, he tries to share his experience in software development through his personal blog at `altanovela.wordpress.com`. You can reach him on Skype at `rio.bastian` or e-mail him at `altanovela@gmail.com`.

Mark Kromer has been working in the database, analytics, and business intelligence industry for 20 years, with a focus on big data and NoSQL since 2011. As a product manager, he has been responsible for the Pentaho MongoDB Analytics product road map for Pentaho, the graph database strategy for DataStax, and the business intelligence road map for Microsoft's vertical solutions. Mark is currently a big data cloud architect and is a frequent contributor to the *TDWI* BI magazine, *MSDN Magazine*, and *SQL Server Magazine*. You can keep up with his speaking and writing schedule at `http://www.kromerbigdata.com`.

www.PacktPub.com

Support files, eBooks, discount offers, and more

For support files and downloads related to your book, please visit www.PacktPub.com.

Did you know that Packt offers eBook versions of every book published, with PDF and ePub files available? You can upgrade to the eBook version at www.PacktPub.com and as a print book customer, you are entitled to a discount on the eBook copy. Get in touch with us at service@packtpub.com for more details.

At www.PacktPub.com, you can also read a collection of free technical articles, sign up for a range of free newsletters and receive exclusive discounts and offers on Packt books and eBooks.

https://www2.packtpub.com/books/subscription/packtlib

Do you need instant solutions to your IT questions? PacktLib is Packt's online digital book library. Here, you can search, access, and read Packt's entire library of books.

Why Subscribe?

- ▶ Fully searchable across every book published by Packt
- ▶ Copy and paste, print, and bookmark content
- ▶ On demand and accessible via a web browser

Free Access for Packt account holders

If you have an account with Packt at www.PacktPub.com, you can use this to access PacktLib today and view 9 entirely free books. Simply use your login credentials for immediate access.

Table of Contents

Preface

With an increasing interest in big data technologies, Pentaho, as a famous open source analysis tool, and MongoDB, the most famous NoSQL database, have gained special focus. The variety of features in Pentaho for MongoDB are end-to-end. This means from data storage in MongoDB clusters to visualization in a dashboard, in a report by e-mail, it's definitely a good change for the processes in enterprises. It's a powerful combination of scalable data storage, data transformation, and analysis.

Pentaho Analytics for MongoDB Cookbook explains the features of Pentaho for MongoDB in detail through clear and practical recipes that you can quickly apply to your solutions. Each chapter guides you through the different components of Pentaho: data integration, OLAP, reporting, dashboards, and analysis. This book is a guide to getting started with Pentaho and provides all of the practical information about the connectivity of Pentaho for MongoDB.

Pentaho Installation

Pentaho is a commercial open source product, which that means there are two versions available: Pentaho Community Edition (CE) and Pentaho Enterprise Edition (EE). To be able to cover all the recipes of this book, please choose Pentaho EE. You can download the trial version, available at `http://www.pentaho.com`. In this book, it is mentioned if a specific feature is available in Pentaho CE. You can get that version from `http://community.pentaho.com`.

Now, we will explain the installation for Pentaho EE:

1. Download the Pentaho EE trial from `http://www.pentaho.com`.

2. Run the `pentaho-business-analytics-<version>.exe` file for a Windows environment or `pentaho-business-analytics-<version>.bin` for a Linux environment. You will get a **Welcome** window, like what is shown in the following screenshot:

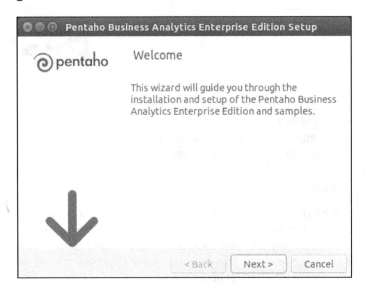

3. Click on **Next** and you will get the license agreement, as shown in this screenshot:

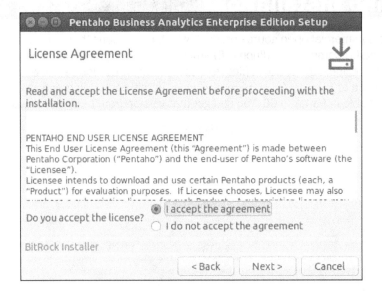

4. After carefully reading the license agreement and accepting, you will be able to choose the setup type in the next screen, as shown in the following screenshot:

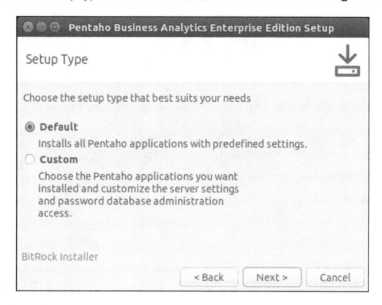

5. In this case, we'll choose a **Default** installation and click on **Next**. You'll be taken to a screen to choose the folder where Pentaho will be installed, as shown in this screenshot:

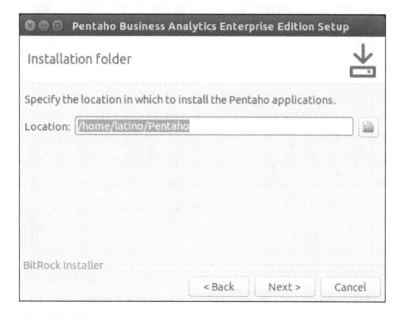

6. Feel free to choose your folder path and click on **Next**. You'll get a screen for setting an administrator password, like this:

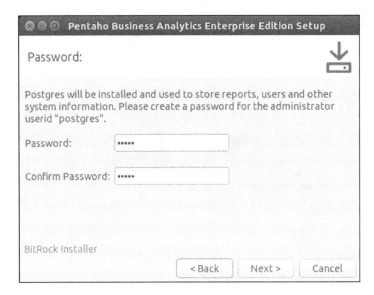

7. After typing your password, click on **Next** and you'll be taken to a **Ready To Install** screen, as shown in the following screenshot. Click on **Next** to start the installation and wait a few minutes.

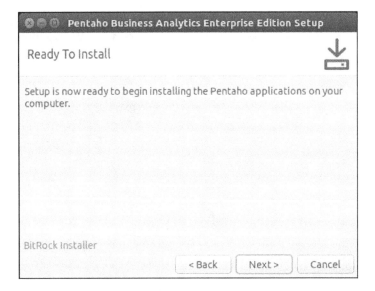

8. After some minutes, you will see a screen saying that the installation is complete, and you can test it by accessing `http://localhost:8080/` from your web browser.

What this book covers

Chapter 1, PDI and MongoDB, introduces Pentaho Data Integration (PDI), which is an ETL tool for extracting, loading, and transforming data from different data sources.

Chapter 2, The Thin Kettle JDBC Driver, teaches you about the JDBC driver for querying Pentaho transformations that connect to various data sources.

Chapter 3, Pentaho Instaview, shows you how to create a quick analysis over MongoDB.

Chapter 4, A MongoDB OLAP Schema, explains how to create and publish Pentaho OLAP schemas from MongoDB.

Chapter 5, Pentaho Reporting, focuses on the creation of printable reports using the Pentaho Report Designer tool. This report can be exported in several formats.

Chapter 6, The Pentaho BI Server, covers the main Pentaho EE plugins for web visualization: Pentaho Analyzer and Pentaho Dashboards Designer.

Chapter 7, Pentaho Dashboards, focuses on the creation of complex dashboards using the open source suite CTools.

Chapter 8, Pentaho Community Contributions, explains the functionality of some contributions from the Pentaho community for MongoDB in Pentaho Data Integration.

What you need for this book

In this book, the software that we need to perform the recipes is:

- ▸ Pentaho Business Analytics v5.3.0
- ▸ MongoDB v2.6.9 (64-bit)

This book provides the source code and some source data for the recipes. Both types of files are available as free downloads from `http://www.packtpub.com/support`.

Who this book is for

This book is primarily intended for MongoDB professionals who are looking for analysis using Pentaho. This can be done to perform business analysis by Pentaho consultants, Pentaho architects, and developers who want to be able to deliver solutions using Pentaho and MongoDB. It is assumed that they already have experience of defining business requirements and knowledge of MongoDB.

Sections

In this book, you will find several headings that appear frequently (Getting ready, How to do it, How it works, There's more, and See also).

To give clear instructions on how to complete a recipe, we use these sections as follows.

Getting ready

This section tells you what to expect in the recipe, and describes how to set up any software or any preliminary settings required for the recipe.

How to do it...

This section contains the steps required to follow the recipe.

How it works...

This section usually consists of a detailed explanation of what happened in the previous section.

There's more...

This section consists of additional information about the recipe in order to make the reader more knowledgeable about the recipe.

See also

This section provides helpful links to other useful information for the recipe.

Conventions

In this book, you will find a number of styles of text that distinguish between different kinds of information. Here are some examples of these styles, and an explanation of their meaning.

A block of code is set as follows:

```
[
    { $match: {"customer.name" : "Baane Mini Imports"} },
    { $group: {"_id" : {"orderNumber": "$orderNumber",
      "orderDate" : "$orderDate"}, "totalSpend": { $sum:
        "$totalPrice"} } }
```

Any command-line input or output is written as follows:

```
db.Orders.find({"priceEach":{$gte:100},"customer.name":"Baane Mini
Imports"}).count()]
```

New terms and **important words** are shown in bold. Words that you see on the screen, for example, in menus or dialog boxes, appear in the text like this: "Set the **Step Name** property to **Select Customers**."

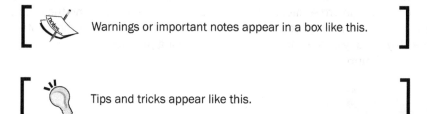

Warnings or important notes appear in a box like this.

Tips and tricks appear like this.

Reader feedback

Feedback from our readers is always welcome. Let us know what you think about this book—what you liked or may have disliked. Reader feedback is important for us to develop titles that you really get the most out of.

To send us general feedback, simply send an e-mail to feedback@packtpub.com, and mention the book title via the subject of your message.

If there is a topic that you have expertise in and you are interested in either writing or contributing to a book, see our author guide on www.packtpub.com/authors.

Customer support

Now that you are the proud owner of a Packt book, we have a number of things to help you to get the most from your purchase.

Downloading the example code

You can download the example code files for all Packt books you have purchased from your account at http://www.packtpub.com. If you purchased this book elsewhere, you can visit http://www.packtpub.com/support and register to have the files e-mailed directly to you.

Errata

Although we have taken every care to ensure the accuracy of our content, mistakes do happen. If you find a mistake in one of our books—maybe a mistake in the text or the code—we would be grateful if you would report this to us. By doing so, you can save other readers from frustration and help us improve subsequent versions of this book. If you find any errata, please report them by visiting http://www.packtpub.com/submit-errata, selecting your book, clicking on the **errata submission form** link, and entering the details of your errata. Once your errata are verified, your submission will be accepted and the errata will be uploaded on our website, or added to any list of existing errata, under the Errata section of that title. Any existing errata can be viewed by selecting your title from http://www.packtpub.com/support.

Piracy

Piracy of copyright material on the Internet is an ongoing problem across all media. At Packt, we take the protection of our copyright and licenses very seriously. If you come across any illegal copies of our works, in any form, on the Internet, please provide us with the location address or website name immediately so that we can pursue a remedy.

Please contact us at copyright@packtpub.com with a link to the suspected pirated material.

We appreciate your help in protecting our authors, and our ability to bring you valuable content.

Questions

You can contact us at questions@packtpub.com if you are having a problem with any aspect of the book, and we will do our best to address it.

1
PDI and MongoDB

In this chapter, we will cover these recipes:

- ▶ Learning basic operations with Pentaho Data Integration
- ▶ Migrating data from the RDBMS to MongoDB
- ▶ Loading data from MongoDB to MySQL
- ▶ Migrating data from files to MongoDB
- ▶ Exporting MongoDB data using the aggregation framework
- ▶ MongoDB Map/Reduce using the User Defined Java Class step and MongoDB Java Driver
- ▶ Working with jobs and filtering MongoDB data using parameters and variables

Introduction

Migrating data from an RDBMS to a NoSQL database, such as MongoDB, isn't an easy task, especially when your RBDMS has a lot of tables. It can be a time consuming issue, and in most cases, using a manual process is like developing a bespoke solution.

Pentaho Data Integration (or PDI, also known as Kettle) is an Extract, Transform, and Load (ETL) tool that can be used as a solution for this problem. PDI provides a graphical drag-and-drop development environment called **Spoon**. Primarily, PDI is used to create data warehouses. However, it can also be used for other scenarios, such as migrating data between two databases, exporting data to files with different formats (flat, CSV, JSON, XML, and so on), loading data into databases from many different types of source data, data cleaning, integrating applications, and so on.

The following recipes will focus on the main operations that you need to know to work with PDI and MongoDB.

Learning basic operations with Pentaho Data Integration

The following recipe is aimed at showing you the basic building blocks that you can use for the rest of the recipes in this chapter. We recommend that you work through this simple recipe before you tackle any of the others. If you want, PDI also contains a large selection of sample transformations for you to open, edit, and test. These can be found in the sample directory of PDI.

Getting ready

Before you can begin this recipe, you will need to make sure that the **JAVA_HOME** environment variable is set properly. By default, PDI tries to guess the value of the **JAVA_HOME** environment variable. Note that for this book, we are using Java 1.7. As soon as this is done, you're ready to launch **Spoon**, the graphical development environment for PDI. To start **Spoon**, you can use the appropriate scripts located at the PDI home folder. To start Spoon in Windows, you will have to execute the **spoon.bat** script in the home folder of PDI. For **Linux** or **Mac**, you will have to execute the **spoon.sh** bash script instead.

How to do it...

First, we need configure Spoon to be able to create transformations and/or jobs. To acclimatize to the tool, perform the following steps:

1. Create a new empty transformation:

   1. Click on the **New file** button from the toolbar menu and select the **Transformation** item entry. You can also navigate to **File | New | Transformation** from the main menu. *Ctrl + N* also creates a new transformation.

2. Set a name for the transformation:

   1. Open the **Transformation settings** dialog by pressing *Ctrl + T*. Alternatively, you can right-click on the right-hand-side working area and select **Transformation settings**. Or on the menu bar, select the **Settings...** item entry from the **Edit** menu.

   2. Select the **Transformation** tab.

   3. Set **Transformation Name** to First Test Transformation.

   4. Click on the **OK** button.

3. Save the transformation:

    1. Click on the **Save current file** button from the toolbar. Alternatively, from the menu bar, go to **File | Save**. Or finally, use the quick option by pressing *Ctrl + S*.

    2. Choose the location of your transformation and give it the name **chapter1-first-transformation**.

    3. Click on the **OK** button.

4. Run a transformation using Spoon.

    1. You can run the transformation by either of these ways: click on the green play icon on the transformation toolbar and navigate to **Action | Run** on the main menu or simply press *F9*.

    2. You will get an **Execute a transformation** dialog. Here, you can set **parameters**, **variables**, or **arguments** if they are required for running the transformation.

    3. Run the transformation by clicking on the **Launch** button.

5. Run the transformation in **preview mode** using Spoon.

    1. In the **Transformation debug** dialog, select the step you want to preview the output data.

    2. After selecting the desired output step, you can preview the transformation by either clicking on the magnify icon on the transformation toolbar, going to **Action | Preview** on the main menu, or simply pressing *F10*.

    3. You will get a **Transformation debug** dialog that you can use to define the number of rows you want to see, breakpoints, and the step that you want analyze.

    4. You can click on the **Configure** button to define **parameters**, **variables**, or **arguments**. Click on the **Quick Launch** button to preview the transformation.

How it works...

In this recipe, we just introduced the Spoon tool, touching on the main basic points for you to manage ETL transformations. We started by creating a transformation. We gave a name to the transformation, `First Test Transformation` in this case. Then, we saved the transformation in the filesystem with the name `chapter1-first-transformation`.

Finally, we ran the transformation normally and in debug mode. Understanding how to run a transformation in debug mode is useful for future ETL developments as it helps you understand what is happening inside of the transformation.

There's more...

In the PDI home folder, you will find a large selection of sample transformations and jobs that you can open, edit, and run to better understand the functionality of the diverse steps available in PDI.

Migrating data from the RDBMS to MongoDB

In this recipe, you will transfer data from a sample RDBMS to a MongoDB database. The sample data is called **SteelWheels** and is available in the Pentaho BA server, running on the Hypersonic Database Server.

Getting ready

Start the Pentaho BA Server by executing the appropriate scripts located in the BA Server's home folder. It is `start-pentaho.sh` for Unix/Linux operating systems, and for the Windows operating system, it is `start-pentaho.bat`. Also in Windows, you can go to the **Start** menu and choose **Pentaho Enterprise Edition**, then **Server Management**, and finally **Start BA Server**.

Start Pentaho Data Integration by executing the right scripts in the PDI home folder. It is `spoon.sh` for Unix/Linux operating systems and `spoon.bat` for the Windows operating system. Besides this, in Windows, you can go to the **Start** menu and choose **Pentaho Enterprise Edition**, then **Design Tools**, and finally **Data Integration**.

Start MongoDB. If you don't have the server running as a service, you need execute the `mongod -dbpath=<data folder>` command in the bin folder of MongoDB.

To make sure you have the Pentaho BA Server started, you can access the default URL, which is `http://localhost:8080/pentaho/`. When you launch Spoon, you should see a welcome screen like the one pictured here:

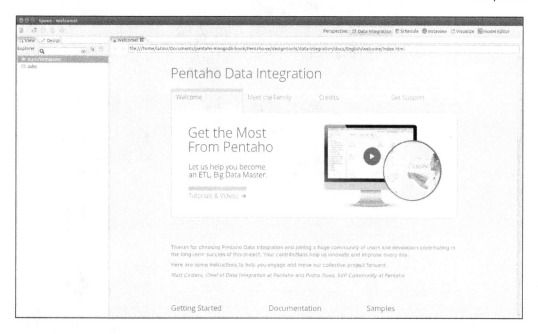

How to do it...

After you have made that sure you are ready to start the recipe, perform the following steps:

1. Create a new empty transformation.

   1. As was explained in the first recipe of this chapter, set the name of this transformation to **Migrate data from RDBMS to MongoDB**.

   2. Save the transformation with the name **chapter1-rdbms-to-mongodb**.

2. Select a customer's data from the **SteelWheels** database using **Table Input** step.

   1. Select the **Design** tab in the left-hand-side view.

   2. From the **Input** category folder, find the **Table Input** step and drag and drop it into the working area in the right-hand-side view.

   3. Double-click on the **Table Input** step to open the configuration dialog.

   4. Set the **Step Name** property to **Select Customers**.

   5. Before we can get any data from the **SteelWheels** Hypersonic database, we will have to create a JDBC connection to it.

      To do this, click on the **New** button next to the **Database Connection** pulldown. This will open the **Database Connection** dialog.

Set **Connection Name** to **SteelWheels**. Next, select the **Connection Type** as **Hypersonic**. Set **Host Name** to **localhost**, **Database Name** to **SampleData**, **Port** to **9001**, **Username** to **pentaho_user**, and finally **Password** to **password**. Your setup should look similar to the following screenshot:

6. You can test the connection by clicking on the **Test** button at the bottom of the dialog. You should get a message similar to **Connection Successful**. If not, then you must double-check your connection details.

7. Click on **OK** to return to the **Table Input** step.

8. Now that we have a valid connection set, we are able to get a list of customers from the **SteelWheels** database. Copy and paste the following SQL into the query text area:

```
SELECT * FROM CUSTOMERs
```

9. Click on the **Preview** button and you will see a table of customer details.

10. Your **Table Input** step configuration should look similar to what is shown in the following screenshot:

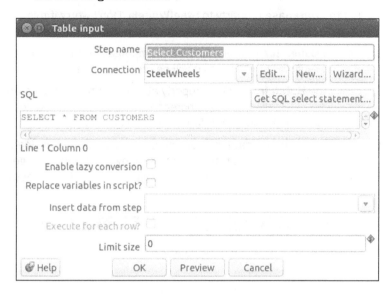

11. Click on **OK** to exit the **Table Input configuration** dialog.

3. Now, let's configure the output of the customer's data in the MongoDB database.

1. Under the **Design** tab, from the **Big Data** category folder, find the **MongoDB Output** step and drag and drop it into the working area in the right-hand-side view.

2. As we want data to flow from the **Table Input** step to the **MongoDB Output** step, we are going to create a **Hop** between the steps. To do this, simply hover over the **Table Input** step and a popup will appear, with some options below the step. Click on **Right Arrow** and then on the **MongoDB Output** step. This will create a **Hop** between the two steps.

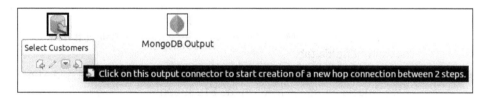

3. It's time to configure the MongoDB Output step. Double-click on it.

4. Set **Step Name** to **Customers Output**.

5. As we're running a default MongoDB instance, we only have to set some simple properties in this step. Set **Hostname** to **localhost** and **Port** to **27017**.

6. Select the **Output options** tab. In this tab, we can define how the data will be inserted into MongoDB.

7. Set the **Database** property to **SteelWheels**. Don't worry if this database doesn't exist in MongoDB, as it will be created automatically.

8. Set the **Collection** property to **Customers.** Again, don't worry if this collection doesn't exist in MongoDB, as it will be created automatically.

9. Leave the **Batch insert size** property at 100. For performance and/or production purposes, you can increase it if necessary. If you don't provide any value to this field, the default value will be 100.

10. We are going to truncate the collection each time before we load data. In this way, if we rerun the transformation many times, we won't get duplicate records. Your **Output options** page should look like what is shown in this screenshot:

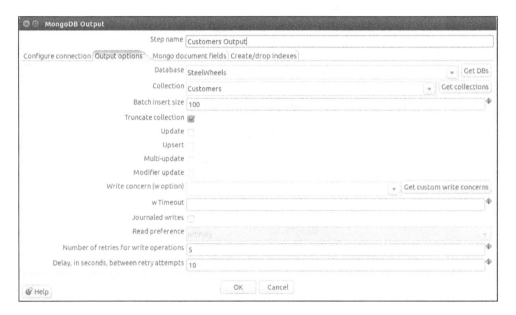

11. Now, let's define the MongoDB documents structure. Select the **Mongo document fields** tab.

12. Click on the **Get fields** button, and the fields list will be populated with the SteelWheels database fields in the ETL stream.

13. By default, the column names in the SteelWheels database are in uppercase. In MongoDB, these field names should be in camel case. You can manually edit the names of the **MongoDB document paths** in this section also. Make sure that the **Use Field Name** option is set to **No** for each field, like this:

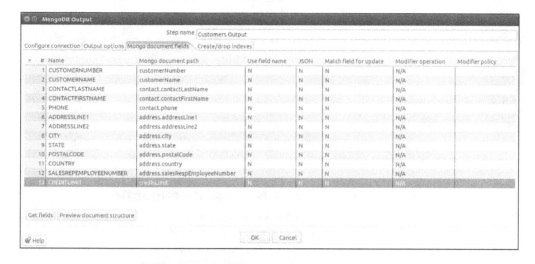

14. By clicking on **Preview document structure**, you will see an example of what the document will look like when it is inserted into the MongoDB **Customers** collection.

15. Click on the **OK** button to finish the MongoDB Output configuration.

4. The transformation design is complete. You can run it for testing purposes using the Run button, as illustrated here:

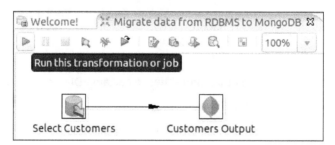

How it works...

As you can see, this is a basic transformation that loads data from the RDBMS database and inserts it into a MongoDB collection. This is a very simple example of loading data from one point to another. Not all transformations are like this. That is why PDI comes with various steps that allow you to manipulate data along the way.

In this case, we truncate the collection each time the transformation is run. However, it is also possible to use other combinations, such as **Insert&Update** or just **Insert** or **Update** individually.

There's more...

Now that we have designed a transformation, let's look at a simple way of reusing the MongoDB connection for future transformations.

How to reuse the properties of a MongoDB connection

If you have to create MongoDB connections manually for each transformation, you are likely to make mistakes and typos. A good way to avoid this is to store the MongoDB connection details in a separate `.properties` file on your filesystem. There is a file called `kettle.properties` that is located in a hidden directory called `.kettle` in your home directory. For example, in Linux, the location will be `/home/latino/.kettle`. In Windows, it will be `C:\Users\latino\.kettle`. Navigate to and open this **.properties** file in your favorite text editor. Then, copy and paste the following lines:

```
MONGODB_STEELWHEELS_HOSTNAME=localhost
MONGODB_STEELWHEELS_PORT=27017
MONGODB_STEELWHEELS_USERNAME=
MONGODB_STEELWHEELS_PASSWORD=
```

Save the **.properties** file and restart Spoon.

Now, where can we use these properties?

You will notice that when you are setting properties in certain PDI steps, you can see the following icon:

This icon denotes that we can use a variable or parameter in place of a static value. Variables are defined using the following structure: **${MY_VARIABLE}**. You will notice that the variables are encapsulated in **${}**. If you are not sure what the name of your variable is, you can also press *Ctrl* and the Spacebar; this will open a drop-down list of the available variables. You will see the MongoDB variables that you defined in the **.properties** file earlier in this list. With this in mind, we can now replace the connection details in our steps with variables as shown in this screenshot:

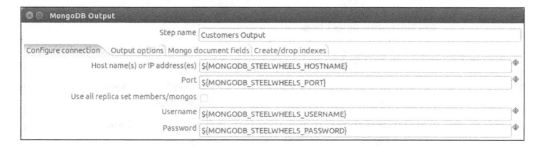

You can find out more about the MongoDB Output step on this documentation website: `http://wiki.pentaho.com/display/EAI/MongoDB+Output`

Loading data from MongoDB to MySQL

In this recipe, we will guide you through extracting data from MongoDB and inserting it into a MySQL database. You will create a simple transformation as you did in the last recipe, but in reverse. You don't have to use MySQL as your database. If you want, you can use any other database. You just need to make sure that you can connect to Pentaho Data Integration via JDBC. However, in this book, we will use MySQL as an example.

Getting ready

Make sure you have created a MySQL database server or some other database type server with a database called SteelWheels. Also make sure that your MongoDB instance is running and launch Spoon.

How to do it...

After you have made sure that you have the databases set up, perform the following steps:

1. Create a new empty transformation.
   1. Set the name for this transformation to **Loading data from MongoDB to MySQL**.
   2. Save the transformation with the name `chapter1-mongodb-to-mysql`.

2. Select **Customers** from MongoDB using the **MongoDB Input** step.

    1. Select the **Design** tab in the left-hand-side view.

    2. From the **Big Data** category folder, find the **MongoDB Input** step and drag and drop it into the working area in the right-hand-side view.

    3. Double-click on the **MongoDB Input** step to open the configuration dialog.

    4. Set the **Step Name** property to **Select Customers**.

    5. Select the **Input options** tab. Click on **Get DBs** and select **SteelWheels** from the **Database** select box.

    6. After selecting the database, you can click on the **Get Collections** button and then select **Customers Collection** from the select box.

    7. As we're just running one MongoDB instance, we'll keep **Read preference** as **primary** and will not configure any **Tag set specification**.

    8. Click on the **Query** tab. In this section, we'll define the **where** filter data condition and the fields that we want to extract.

    9. As we just want the customers from USA, we'll write the following query in the **Query expression (JSON)** field: {"address.country": "USA"}.

 In this recipe, we are not going to cover the MongoDB aggregation framework, so you can ignore those options for now.

    10. Click on the **Fields** tab. In this tab, we'll define the output fields that we want. By default, the **Output single JSON** field comes checked. This means that each document is extracted in the **JSON** format with the field name defined in the **Name of JSON output field**. As we want to define the fields, we remove the selection of the **Output single JSON field**.

    11. Click on the **Get fields** button and you will get all the fields available from MongoDB. Remove the **_id** field because it isn't necessary. For deletion, you can select the row of the **_id** field and press the **Delete** key from your keyboard, or right-click on the row and select the **Delete selected lines** option.

    12. Click on **OK** to finish the **MongoDB Input** configuration.

3. Let's configure the output of the MongoDB **Customers** data in the MySQL database.

    1. On the **Design** tab, from the **Output** category folder, find the **Table Output** step and drag and drop it into the working area in the right-hand-side view.

    2. Connect the **MongoDB Input** step to the **Table output** step by creating a hop between them.

3. Double-click on the step to open the **Table Output** configuration dialog.

4. Set **Step Name** to **Customers Output**.

5. Click on the **New** button next to the **Database Connection** pulldown. This will open the **Database Connection** dialog.

   Set **Connection Name** to **SteelWheels**. Select the **Connection Type** as **MySQL**. Set **Host Name** to **localhost**, **Database Name** to **SteelWheels**, and **Port** to **3306**. Then, set **Username** and **Password** to whatever you had set them as. Your setup should look similar to the following screenshot:

6. Test this, and if all is well, click on **OK** to return to the **Table Output** step.

4. Insert this data into a MySQL table using the **Table Output** step:

   1. Set the **Target table** field to **Customers**. This is the name of the MySQL table to insert data into.

   2. As we haven't created a customer's table in the MySQL database, we can use a PDI function that will try to generate the required SQL to create the table and structure. Simply click on the **SQL** button and it will open the **Execute SQL** dialog. Here, you will see the SQL that PDI will execute to create the customers table. Click on **Execute** to send this SQL to MySQL and create the table. Then, click on **OK.**

   3. Click on **OK** again to exit the **Table Output** configuration dialog. The transformation is complete. You can now run it to load data from MongoDB to MySQL.

How it works...

In this transformation, we are simply selecting a collection from the MongoDB Input step where the country field is USA. Next, we map this collection to the fields in the PDI stream. Lastly, we insert this data into a MySQL table using the Table Output step. In the **Fields** tab, we use JSONPath to select the correct data from the MongoDB collection (`http://goessner.net/articles/JsonPath/`). JSONPath is like XPath for JSON documents.

Migrating data from files to MongoDB

In this recipe, we will guide you through creating a transformation that loads data from different files in your filesystem, and then load them into a MongoDB Collection. We are going to load data from files called **orders.csv**, **customers.xls**, and **products.xml**. Each of these files contains a key that we can use to join data in PDI before we send it to the MongoDB Output step.

Getting ready

Start Spoon and take a look at the content of the `orders.csv`, `customers.xls`, and `products.xml` files. This will help you understand what the data looks like before you start loading it into MongoDB.

How to do it...

You will need the `orders.csv`, `customers.xls`, and `products.xml` files. These files will be available at the Packt Publishing website, just in case you don't have them. Make sure that MongoDB is up and running, and then you will be able to perform to the following steps:

1. Create a new empty transformation.

    1. Set the transformation name to **Migrate data from files to MongoDB**.

    2. Save the transformation with the name **chapter1-files-to-mongodb**.

2. Select data from the **orders.csv** file using the **CSV file input** step.

    1. Select the **Design** tab in the left-hand-side view.

    2. From the **Input** category folder, find the **CSV file input** step and drag and drop it into the working area in the right-hand-side view.

    3. Double-click on the step to open the **CSV Input** configuration dialog.

4. Set **Step Name** to **Select Orders**.

5. In the **Filename** field, click on the **Browse** button, navigate to the location of the `.csv` file, and select the **order.csv** file.

6. Set the **Delimiter** field to a semicolon (`;`).

7. Now, let's define our output fields by clicking on the **Get Fields** button. A **Sample size** dialog will appear; it is used to analyze the format data in the CSV file. Click on **OK**. Then, click on **Close** in **Scan results**.

8. Click on **OK** to finish the configuration of the **CSV file input**.

3. Select data from the **customers.xls** file using the **Microsoft Excel Input** step.

   1. Select the **Design** tab in the left-hand-side view.

   2. From the **Input** category folder, find the **Microsoft Excel Input** step and drag and drop it into the working area in the right-hand-side view.

   3. Double-click on the step to open the **Microsoft Excel Input** dialog.

   4. Set **Step Name** to **Select Customers**.

   5. On the **Files** tab, in the **File or directory** field, click on the **Browse** button and choose the location of the **customers.xls** file in your filesystem. After that, click on the **Add** button to add the file to the list of files to be processed.

   6. Select the **Sheets** tab. Then, click on the **Get sheetname(s)...** button. You'll be shown an **Enter list** dialog. Select **Sheet1** and click on the **>** button to add a sheet to the **Your selection** list. Finally, click on **OK**.

   7. Select the **Fields** tab. Then, click on the **Get field from header row...** button. This will generate a list of existing fields in the spreadsheet. You will have to make a small change; change the **Type** field for **Customer Number** from **Number** to **Integer**. You can preview the file data by clicking on the **Preview rows** button.

   8. Click on **OK** to finish the configuration of the **Select Customers step**.

4. Select data from the **products.xml** file using the **Get data from XML** step.

   1. Select the **Design** tab in the left-hand-side view.

   2. From the **Input** category folder, find the **Get data from XML** step and drag and drop it into the working area in the right-hand-side view.

   3. Double-click on the step to open the **Get data from XML** dialog.

   4. Set **Step Name** to **Select Products**.

   5. On the **File** tab, in the **File or directory** field, click on the **Browse** button and choose the location of the **products.xml** file in your filesystem. After that, click on the **Add** button to add the file to the list of files to be processed.

   6. Select the **Content** tab. Click on the **Get XPath nodes** button and select the **/products/product** option from the list of the **Available Paths** dialog.

7. Next, select the **Fields** tab. Click on the **Get fields** button and you will get a list of available fields in the XML file. Change the types of the last three fields (**stockquantity, buyprice,** and **MSRP**) from **Number** to **Integer**. Set the **Trim Type** to **Both** for all fields.

5. Now, let's join the data from the three different files.

    1. Select the **Design** tab in the left-hand-side view.

    2. From the **Lookup** category folder, find the **Stream lookup** step. Drag and drop it onto the working area in the right-hand-side view. Double-click on **Stream lookup** and change the **Step name** field to **Lookup Customers**.

    3. We are going to need two lookup steps for this transformation. Drag and drop another Stream Lookup step onto the design view, and set **Step Name** to **Lookup Products**.

    4. Create a hop between the **Select Orders** step and the **Lookup Customers** step.

    5. Then, create a hop from the **Select Customers** step to the **Lookup Customers** step.

    6. Next, create a hop from the **Lookup Customers** step to the **Lookup Products** step.

    7. Finally, create a hop from **Select Products** to the **Lookup Products** step.

6. Let's configure the **Lookup Customers** step. Double-click on the **Lookup Customers** step and set the **Lookup step** field to the **Select Customers** option.

    1. In the **Keys** section, set the **Field** and **Lookup Field** options to **Customer Number**.

    2. Click on the **Get lookup fields** button. This will populate the step with all the available fields from the lookup source. Remove **Customer Number** from the field from the list.

    3. Click on **OK** to finish.

7. Let's configure the **Lookup Products** step. The process is similar to that of the **Lookup Customers** step but with different values. Double-click on the **Lookup Products** step and set the **Lookup step** field to the **Select Products** option.

    1. In the **Keys** section, set **Field** to **Product Code** and the **LookupField** option to **Code**.

    2. Click on the **Get lookup fields** button. This will populate the step with all the available fields from the lookup source. Remove **Code** from the field in the list.

    3. Click on **OK** to finish.

8. Now that we have the data joined correctly, we can write the data stream to a MongoDB collection.

    1. On the **Design** tab, from the **Big Data** category folder, find the **MongoDB Output** step and drag and drop it into the working area in the right-hand-side view.

    2. Create a hop between the **Lookup Products** step and the **MongoDB Output** step.

    3. Double-click on the **MongoDB Output** step and change the **Step name** field to **Orders Output**.

    4. Select the **Output options** tab. Click on the **Get DBs** buttons and select the **SteelWheels** option for the **Database** field. Set the **Collection** field to **Orders**. Check the **Truncate collection** option.

    5. Select the **Mongo document fields** tab. Click on the **Get fields** button and you will get a list of fields from the previous step.

    6. Configure the Mongo document output as seen in the following screenshot:

#	Name	Mongo document path	Use field name	JSON	Match field for update	Modifier operation	Modifier policy
1	Order Number	orderNumber	N	N	N	N/A	
2	Quantity Ordered	quantityOrdered	N	N	N	N/A	
3	Price Each	priceEach	N	N	N	N/A	
4	Order Line Number	orderLineNumber	N	N	N	N/A	
5	Total Price	totalPrice	N	N	N	N/A	
6	Order Date	orderDate	N	N	N	N/A	
7	Required Date	requiredDate	N	N	N	N/A	
8	Shipped Date	shippedDate	N	N	N	N/A	
9	Status	status	N	N	N	N/A	
10	Customer Number	customer.customerNumber	N	N	N	N/A	
11	Time	customer.time	N	N	N	N/A	
12	Customer Name	customer.name	N	N	N	N/A	
13	Contact First Name	customer.contact.firstName	N	N	N	N/A	
14	Contact Last Name	customer.contact.lastName	N	N	N	N/A	
15	Phone	customer.contact.phone	N	N	N	N/A	
16	Address Line 1	customer.address.addressLine1	N	N	N	N/A	
17	Address Line 2	customer.address.addressLine2	N	N	N	N/A	
18	City	customer.address.city	N	N	N	N/A	
19	State	customer.address.state	N	N	N	N/A	
20	Postal Code	customer.address.postalCode	N	N	N	N/A	
21	Country	customer.address.country	N	N	N	N/A	
22	Sales Rep Employee Number	customer.salesRepEmployeeNumber	N	N	N	N/A	
23	Credit Limit	customer.creditLimit	N	N	N	N/A	
24	Product Code	product.code	N	N	N	N/A	
25	name	product.name	N	N	N	N/A	
26	line	product.line	N	N	N	N/A	
27	scale	product.scale	N	N	N	N/A	
28	vendor	product.vendor	N	N	N	N/A	
29	description	product.description	N	N	N	N/A	
30	stockquantity	product.stockquantity	N	N	N	N/A	
31	buyprice	product.buyprice	N	N	N	N/A	
32	MSRP	product.msrp	N	N	N	N/A	

    7. Click on **OK.**

9. You can run the transformation and check out MongoDB for the new data. Your transformation should look like the one in this screenshot:

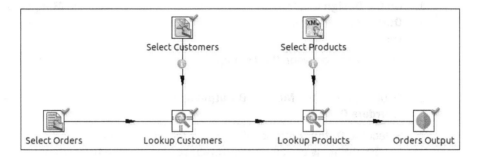

How it works...

In this transformation, we initially get data from the Orders CSV. This first step populates the primary data stream in PDI. Our other XLS and XML steps also collect data. We then connect these two streams of data to the first stream using the Lookup steps and the correct keys. When we finally have all of the data in the single stream, we can load it into the MongoDB collection.

You can learn more about the **Stream lookup** step online at:

`http://wiki.pentaho.com/display/EAI/Stream+Lookup`

Exporting MongoDB data using the aggregation framework

In this recipe, we will explore the use of the MongoDB aggregation framework in the MongoDB Input Step. We will create a simple example to get data from a collection and show you how you can take advantage of the MongoDB aggregation framework to prepare data for the PDI stream.

Getting ready

To get ready for this recipe, you will need to start your ETL development environment **Spoon**, and make sure that you have the MongoDB server running with the data from the previous recipe.

How to do it...

The following steps introduce the use of the MongoDB aggregation framework:

1. Create a new empty transformation.

    1. Set the transformation to **PDI using MongoDB Aggregation Framework**.

    2. Set the name for this transformation to `chapter1-using-mongodb-aggregation-framework`.

2. Select data from the **Orders** collection using **the MongoDB Input** step.

    1. Select the **Design** tab in the left-hand-side view.

    2. From the **Big Data** category folder, find the **MongoDB Input** step and drag and drop it into the working area in the right-hand-side view.

    3. Double-click on the step to open the **MongoDB Input** dialog.

    4. Set the step name to **Select 'Baane Mini Imports' Orders**.

    5. Select the **Input options** tab. Click on the **Get DBs** button and select the **SteelWheels** option for the **Database** field. Next, click on **Get collections** and select the **Orders** option for the **Collection** field.

    6. Select the **Query** tab and then check the **Query is aggregation pipeline** option. In the text area, write the following aggregation query:

       ```
       [
       { $match: {"customer.name" : "Baane Mini Imports"} },
       { $group: {"_id" : {"orderNumber": "$orderNumber",
       "orderDate" : "$orderDate"}, "totalSpend": { $sum:
       "$totalPrice"} } }
       ]
       ```

    7. Uncheck the **Output single JSON field** option.

    8. Select the **Fields** tab. Click on the **Get Fields** button and you will get a list of fields returned by the query. You can preview your data by clicking on the Preview button.

    9. Click on the **OK** button to finish the configuration of this step.

3. We want to add a **Dummy** step to the stream. This step does nothing, but it will allow us to select a step to preview our data. Add the **Dummy** step from the **Flow** category to the workspace and name it **OUTPUT**.

4. Create a hop between the **Select 'Baane Mini Imports' Orders** step and the **OUTPUT** step.

5. Select the **OUTPUT** dummy step and preview the data.

How it works...

The MongoDB aggregation framework allows you to define a sequence of operations or stages that is executed in pipeline much like the Unix command-line pipeline. You can manipulate your collection data using operations such as filtering, grouping, and sorting before the data even enters the PDI stream.

In this case, we are using the MongoDB Input step to execute an aggregation framework query. Technically, this does the same as **db.collection.aggregate()**. The query that we execute is broken down into two parts. For the first part, we filter the data based on a customer name. In this case, it is **Baane Mini Imports**. For the second part, we group the data by order number and order date and sum the total price.

See also

In the next recipe, we will talk about other ways in which you can aggregate data using MongoDB Map/Reduce.

MongoDB Map/Reduce using the User Defined Java Class step and MongoDB Java Driver

In this recipe, we will use the MongoDB Map/Reduce on PDI. Unfortunately, PDI doesn't provide a step for this MongoDB feature. However, PDI does provide a step called **User Defined Java Class** (**UDJC**) that will allow you to write Java code to manipulate your data.

We are going to get the total price for all orders for a single client, which we will pass to the transformation as a parameter. We will also get a total for all other clients in the collection. In total, we should get two rows back.

Getting ready

To get ready for this recipe, you need to download the MongoDB driver. In this case, we are using the `mongo-java-driver-2.11.1` version. You can use the last version, but the code in this recipe may be a bit out of date. The driver should live in the **lib** folder of PDI. Then, you just need start your ETL development environment **Spoon** and make sure you have the MongoDB server started with the data from the last recipe inserted.

How to do it...

In this recipe, we'll program Java code and utilize the MongoDB Java driver to connect to the MongoDB database. So, make sure you have the driver in the `lib` folder of PDI and then perform the following steps:

1. Create a new empty transformation.

    1. Set the transformation name to **MongoDB Map/Reduce**.

    2. On the **Transformation properties and Parameters** tab, create a new parameter with the name as **CUSTOMER_NAME**.

    3. Save the transformation with the name **chapter1-mongodb-map-reduce**.

2. From the **Job** category folder, find the **Get Variables** step and drag and drop it into the working area in the right-side view.

    1. Double-click on the **Get Variables** step to open the configuration dialog.

    2. Set the **Step name** property to **Get Customer Name**.

    3. Add a row with the name as **customerName**, the variable as **${CUSTOMER_NAME}**, and **Type set** to **String**.

3. From the **Scripting** category folder, find the **User Defined Java Class** step and drag and drop it into the working area in the right-hand-side view.

4. Create a hop between the **Get Customer Name** step and the **User Defined Java Class** step.

    1. Double-click on the **User Defined Java Class** step to open the configuration dialog.

    2. In the **Step name** field, give a suggested name of **MapReduce**.

    3. In **Class** code, let's define our Java code that is sent to MongoDB by a command using the `MapReduce` functions and then we will get the result:
       ```java
       import com.mongodb.DB;
       import com.mongodb.DBCollection;
       import com.mongodb.DBObject;
       import com.mongodb.MapReduceCommand;
       import com.mongodb.MapReduceOutput;
       import com.mongodb.Mongo;

       private FieldHelper customerNameIn = null;

       public boolean processRow(StepMetaInterface smi,
       StepDataInterface
         sdi) throws KettleException
       {
         Object[] r = getRow();
       ```

```java
    if (r == null) {
      setOutputDone();
      return false;
    }
     if (first) {
      first = false;
      customerNameIn = get(Fields.In, "customerName");
    }

   try {
      final Mongo mongo = new Mongo("localhost", 27017);
      final DB db = mongo.getDB("SteelWheels");
      final DBCollection ordersCol =
db.getCollection("Orders");
      final String map = "function() { "+
        "var category; " +
          "if ( this.customer.name ==
            '"+customerNameIn.getString(r)+"' ) "+
              "category = '"+customerNameIn.
getString(r)+"'; " +
                  "else " + "category = 'Others'; "+
                    "emit(category, {totalPrice: this.
totalPrice,
                      count: 1});}";
      final String reduce = "function(key, values) { " +
        "var n = { count: 0, totalPrice: 0}; " +
          "for ( var i = 0; i < values.length; i++ ) {" +
            "n.count += values[i].count; "+
              "n.totalPrice += values[i].totalPrice; "+
          } " + "return n;} ";
      final MapReduceCommand cmd = new MapReduceCommand(
        ordersCol, map, reduce, null,
          MapReduceCommand.OutputType.INLINE, null);
      final MapReduceOutput out = ordersCol.mapReduce(cmd);
      get(Fields.Out, "mapReduceJSON").setValue(r,out.
toString());
      } catch (Exception e) {
        e.printStackTrace();
        get(Fields.Out, "mapReduceJSON").setValue(r,"");
      }
      r = createOutputRow(r, data.outputRowMeta.size());
      putRow(data.outputRowMeta, r);
      return true;
    }
```

4. On the **Fields** tab, set **Fieldname** to **mapReduceJSON** and the **Type** property to **String**. This will be the field output from the `MapReduce` command.

    5. Click on **OK** to finish the configuration.

5. From the **Input** category folder, find the **Json Input** step and drag and drop it into the working area in the right-hand-side view.

6. Create a hop between the **MapReduce** step and the **Json Input** step.

    1. Double-click on the **JSON Input** step to open the configuration dialog.

    2. Set the **Step Name** property to **Convert JSON**.

    3. On the **File** tab, check the **Source is defined in a field?** option. Next, select the **mapReduceJSON** option in the select box of **Get source from field**.

    4. On the **Fields** tab, we will map the JSON to Fields in the PDI stream. The definition should be like what is shown in this screenshot:

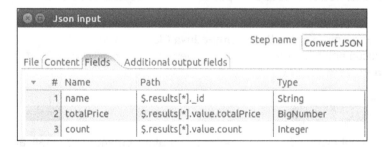

    5. Click on **OK** to finish the configuration.

7. Now, let's define the fields that we want to see as the output of the transformation. From the **Transform** category folder, find the **Select values** step and drag and drop it into the working area in the right-side view.

8. Create a hop between the **Convert JSON** step and the **Select values** step.

    1. Double-click on the **Select Values** step to open the configuration dialog.

    2. Set the **Step Name** property to **OUTPUT**.

3. On the **Select & Alter** tab, click on the **Get fields to select** button. This will populate the table with all the available fields in the stream. Remove the **mapReduceJSON** field; it isn't necessary anymore, since we have converted it into individual fields in the PDI stream.

4. Click on **OK** to finish the configuration.

9. When you run the transformation, be sure to set the **CUSTOMER_NAME** parameter in the **Run** dialog. This will be used by the **Get Customer Name** step and to filter the map function.

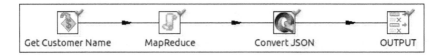

How it works...

In this example, we executed a transformation that takes **CUSTOMER_NAME** as a parameter. This value is then sent to **User Defined Java Class** and used in the Java code within. The code in User Defined Java Class is a simple Map and Reduce JavaScript function that we are sending to the MongoDB server.

The output of this step is a single JSON row that needs to be parsed into fields in the PDI Stream. To do this, we used the JSON input step and mapped the JSON string to individual stream fields.

If you want to know more about **User Defined Java Class**, you can find out more in the documentation at `http://wiki.pentaho.com/display/EAI/User+Defined+Java+Class`.

There's more...

When we talk about map and reduce functions, it is almost mandatory to talk about **Hadoop,** an open source software framework for storage and processing of datasets that uses a MapReduce engine.

PDI provides integration with **Hadoop** using PDI job steps and transformation steps. You can find more documentation about this on the Pentaho website. Personally, I recommend these two tutorials:

▸ `http://wiki.pentaho.com/display/BAD/Using+Pentaho+MapReduce+to+Parse+Weblog+Data`

▸ `http://wiki.pentaho.com/display/BAD/Using+Pentaho+MapReduce+to+Generate+an+Aggregate+Dataset`

Working with jobs and filtering MongoDB data using parameters and variables

In this recipe, we guide you through creating two PDI jobs. One uses variables and the other uses parameters. In a PDI process, jobs orchestrate other jobs and transformations in a coordinated way to realize the main business process. These jobs use the transformation created in the last recipe but with some changes, as described in this recipe.

So, in this recipe, we are going create two different jobs, which will be used to send data to a subtransformation. The subtransformation that we will use will be a copy of the transformation in the previous recipe.

Getting ready

To get ready for this recipe, you need to start your ETL development environment **Spoon**, and make sure you have the MongoDB server started with the data inserted in the last recipes.

How to do it...

Let's start using jobs and variables. We can orchestrate the ETL to run in different ways. In this simple case, we are just using the customer name. Perform the following steps:

1. Let's copy and paste the transformation created in the previous recipe and save it as `chapter1-mongodb-map-reduce-writelog.ktr`.

2. Open that transformation using Spoon, and from the **Utility** category folder, find the **Write to log** step. Drag and drop it into the working area in the right-side view.

   1. Create a hop between the **OUTPUT** step and the **Write to log** step.

   2. Double-click on the **Write to Log** step to open the configuration dialog.

   3. Set **Step Name** to **MapReduce**.

   4. Click on the **Get Fields** button.

   5. Click on **OK** to finish the configuration.

3. Let's create a new empty **job**.

   1. Click on the **New file** button from the toolbar menu and select the **Job** item entry. Alternatively from menu bar, go to **File | New | Job.**

   2. Open the **Job properties** dialog by pressing *Ctrl + J* or by right-clicking on the right-hand-side working area and selecting **Job settings**.

   3. Select the **Job** tab. Set **Job Name** to **Job Parameters**.

4. Select the **Parameters** tab and add a **Parameter** entry with the name as **CUSTOMER_NAME**. Click on **OK**.

5. Save the Job with the name **job-parameters**.

4. From the **General** category folder, find the **START, Transformation**, and **Success** steps and drag and drop them into the working area in the right-side view.

   1. Create a hop between the **START** step and the **Transformation** step.

   2. Then, create a hop from the **Transformation** step to the **Success** step.

   3. Double-click on the **Transformation** step to open the configuration dialog

   4. Change the **Name of job entry** property to **MapReduce Transf**.

   5. Click on the transformation button of the **Transformation filename** field and select the transformation file that you copied before in your filesystem. Also select the **chapter1-mongodb-map-reduce-writelog.ktr** file.

   6. Select the **Parameters** tab. By default, the **Pass all parameters values down to the sub-transformation** option is checked, which means our job parameter will be passed to the transformation.

   7. Click on **OK** to finish.

   8. Run the job and analyze the results and check the logs on the **Logging** tab.

Now let's do a quick and simple example using variables:

1. Copy and paste the `chapter1-mongodb-map-reduce-writelog` transformation. Save it as `chapter1-mongodb-map-reduce-writelog-without-parameter`.

2. Open the transformation with Spoon and remove the parameter from **Transformation properties.**

3. Copy and paste the last job. Save it as `job-variables`.

   1. Open the job with Spoon.

   2. In **Job properties**, change the job name to **Job Variables**. From the **Parameters** tab, remove the **CUSTOMER_NAME** parameter. Select the parameter, right-click on it and select **Delete selected lines**, or just press *delete* on your keyboard.

   3. Click on **OK** to finish.

4. From the **General** category folder, find the **Set variables** step and drag and drop it into the working area in the right-side view.

   1. Remove the hop from between the **START** step and **MapReduce Transf** step.

   2. Create a hop between the **START** step and the **Set variables** step.

3. Then, create a hop between **Set Variables** and the **MapReduce Transf** step.

4. Double-click on the **Set Variables** step to open the configuration dialog.

5. Set the **Step name** property to **Set CUSTOMER_NAME**.

6. On **Variables**, create a new variable with the **CUSTOMER_NAME** name. Set the value to an existing client in the database and the **Scope** type to **Valid in the root job**.

7. Click on **OK** to finish the configuration.

5. On the **MapReduce Transf** transformation step, change the file location for the transformation file to the transformation without the parameter.

6. Run the job and analyze the results, checking the logs in the **Logging** tab.

How it works...

Most ETL solutions created in Pentaho Data Integration will be sets of jobs and transformations.

Transformations are workflows with an orchestration of actions that manipulate data using essentially input, transformation, and output steps.

Jobs are workflows with an orchestration of tasks that can be `order` execution failure or success.

Variables and parameters are extremely useful functions that we can use to create dynamic jobs and transformations.

2

The Thin Kettle
JDBC Driver

In this chapter, we will cover the following recipes:

- ▶ Using a transformation as a data service
- ▶ Running the Carte server in a single instance
- ▶ Running the Pentaho Data Integration server in a single instance
- ▶ Defining a connection using a SQL Client (SQuirreL SQL)

Introduction

The Thin Kettle JDBC Driver provides a means for a Java-based client to query the results of a transformation.

It is a new concept pioneered by *Matt Casters*, (@mattcasters), the Chief Architect of Data Integration at Pentaho and Kettle project founder. It allows any Java-based, JDBC-compliant tool, including third-party reporting systems, to execute a query against a predefined Kettle transformation. This works a lot like a traditional SQL query. The user connects to a thin JDBC data source (Transformation) and sends a SQL query to the data source. The transformation is executed based on the SQL query, and a result set is returned.

 The Thin Kettle JDBC Driver is a feature that is available only in Pentaho Enterprise Edition since version 5.0.

In this chapter, we will teach you how to use the Thin Kettle JDBC Driver with the Carte and Data Integration servers. As with the rest of the book, we will be using Pentaho Enterprise Edition 5.4. The following diagram shows the Just in Time Blending:

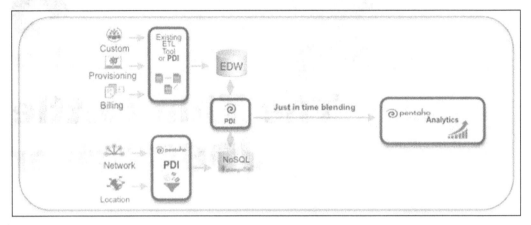

Source: Just in Time Blending from the Pentaho Wiki page

Using a transformation as a data service

This recipe guides you through the process of turning an existing Kettle transformation into a data service for the Thin Kettle JDBC Driver. A data service is a configuration that allows the user to query a transformation as if it were a table in a database.

Getting ready

To get ready for this recipe, you first need to start Spoon and the MongoDB server with the same database from the previous chapter.

How to do it...

We are assuming that you have MongoDB with the data generated in the previous chapters and Spoon open from the Pentaho EE version. Perform the following steps to create a data service:

1. Open the `chapter1-using-mongodb-aggregation-framework.ktr` file and save it as `chapter2-using-mongodb-aggregation-framework-kettle-thin.ktr`. Change the transformation name to `MongoDB Aggregation Kettle Thin`.

2. Define a **Data Service** for this new transformation.

    1. Open the **Transformation settings** dialog. There are two ways of doing this. One is to press *Ctrl + T*, right-click on the right-hand side working area, and select **Transformation settings**. The other is as follows: on the menu bar, select the **Settings...** item entry from **Edit** menu.

2. Select the **Data Service** tab.

3. Click on the **Create new Data Service** button.

4. Set the new virtual table to **AggregationTable.**

5. Click on the **OK** button.

6. Select the **OUTPUT** option of the **Service step** dropdown menu.

3. Click on the **OK** button of the **Transformation properties** dialog and save the transformation.

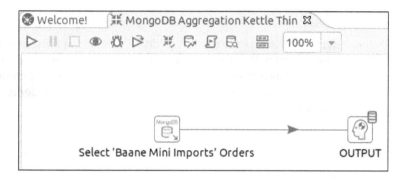

How it works...

As we explained in the previous chapter, this transformation will query data from a MongoDB instance using the MongoDB Aggregation Framework.

However, in this recipe, we configured the output of this transformation to serve as a Kettle Data Service. The configuration for this Kettle Data Service will be saved in the `<user home folder>/.pentaho/metastore/pentaho/Kettle Data Service/` folder with the name as `AggregationTable.xml` in Unix/Linux operating systems and `C:\Users\<user home folder>\.pentaho\metastore\pentaho\Kettle Data Service\AggregationTable.xml`. This XML contains the metadata that describes the data service.

In the next recipes, we will guide you through running Carte and Pentaho Data Integration Server (DI Server) in a single instance/server. You can run these platforms in a cluster, but that isn't the goal of this book. With Carte or DI Server up and running, you will be able to list all details of all Data Services from these documents.

See also

In the next recipe, we will guide you through making the Carte server run, with the data services of Thin Kettle available.

Running the Carte server in a single instance

This recipe guides you through starting a Carte server on a single-instance machine. The Carte server is a lightweight web server that enables remote execution of transformations and jobs. It is a crucial tool for coordinating job and transformation executions in a scale-out cluster environment.

Getting ready

To get ready for this recipe, you first need to start the MongoDB server with the same database as that of the last chapter. You will also have to check `<user home folder>/.pentaho/metastore` in Unix/Linux operating systems, and in the Windows operating system, the `C:\Users\<user home folder>\.pentaho\metastore` folder is accessible to the Carte server.

How to do it...

To start the Carte Server, perform the following steps:

1. First, we will have to configure the properties of Carte Server, such as `hostname`, `port`, and whether it is the `master` in the cluster environment:

    1. You need create an XML file with the following content:

        ```
        <slave_config>
          <slaveserver>
            <name>master</name>
            <hostname>localhost</hostname>
            <port>8082</port>
            <master>Y</master>
          </slaveserver>
        </slave_config>
        ```

    2. Save the file somewhere on your filesystem with the name `carte-config-master-8082.xml`.

2. Open a command-line tool on your operating system and navigate to the `<pentaho-installation-path>/design-tools/data-integration` folder.

3. Start the Carte server by executing the following command:

    ❑   For Unix/Linux operating systems: `./carte.sh <file-path>/carte-config-master-8082.xml`

    ❑   For the Windows operating system: `carte.bat <file-path>/carte-config-master-8082.xml`

4. You should see a message similar to **Carte - Created listener for webserver @ address: localhost:8082** once the server is ready.

5. Open your web browser and navigate to `http://localhost:8082/`.

6. By default, both the username and password are `cluster`. If you wish, you can change the authentication details in the `<pentaho-installation-path>/design-tools/data-integration/pwd/kettle.pwd` file.

7. You can list the available Kettle Data Services by navigating to the `http://localhost:8082/kettle/listServices/` endpoint. You should get a result similar to the following screenshot:

```
            localhost:8082/kettle/listServices/

This XML file does not appear to have any style information associated with it. T

-<services>
 -<service>
    <name>AggregationTable</name>
  -<row-meta>
   -<value-meta>
      <type>Number</type>
      <storagetype>normal</storagetype>
      <name>totalSpend</name>
      <length>-1</length>
      <precision>-1</precision>
      <origin>Select 'Baane Mini Imports' Orders</origin>
      <comments/>
      <conversion_Mask/>
      <decimal_symbol>.</decimal_symbol>
      <grouping_symbol>,</grouping_symbol>
      <currency_symbol/>
      <trim_type>none</trim_type>
      <case_insensitive>N</case_insensitive>
      <sort_descending>N</sort_descending>
      <output_padding>N</output_padding>
      <date_format_lenient>N</date_format_lenient>
      <date_format_locale>en_GB</date_format_locale>
      <date_format_timezone>Europe/London</date_format_timezone>
      <lenient_string_to_number>N</lenient_string_to_number>
    </value-meta>
   -<value-meta>
      <type>Integer</type>
      <storagetype>normal</storagetype>
      <name>orderNumber</name>
      <length>-1</length>
      <precision>-1</precision>
      <origin>Select 'Baane Mini Imports' Orders</origin>
      <comments/>
      <conversion_Mask/>
      <decimal_symbol>.</decimal_symbol>
      <grouping_symbol>,</grouping_symbol>
      <currency_symbol/>
      <trim_type>none</trim_type>
      <case_insensitive>N</case_insensitive>
      <sort_descending>N</sort_descending>
      <output_padding>N</output_padding>
      <date_format_lenient>N</date_format_lenient>
```

How it works...

In this recipe, we created an XML file that was used to configure a single Carte instance. We set the Carte server to run on the local machine on port `8082`. We also set the Carte instance to be the master instance.

To connect to the Carte server, we opened our web browser, navigated to the Carte server and entered our username and password, which were configured in the `<pentaho-installation-path>/design-tools/data-integration/pwd/kettle.pwd` file. The file structure is based in a line with `<username>` : `<password>`. By default, you can see the last line with the password obfuscated:

```
cluster: OBF:1v8w1uh21z7k1ym71z7i1ugo1v9q
```

It is advised that you configure the carte server password to something other than the default in a production environment. It's possible to set the username and password in plain text, but you should instead use `<pentaho-installation-path>/design-tools/data-integration/encr.sh` for Unix/Linux operating systems or `<pentaho-installation-path>/design-tools/data-integration/Encr.bat` for Windows operation systems to set the password.

To set the password, you have to execute the following:

`sh encr.sh -carte carteServerPassword`

`OBF:1shq1uum1xmq1zlo1vu91s9r1sar1rj51z0j1t331z0b1rh91saj1sbj1vv11zlu1xmk1 uvk1shs`

Finally, we listed the available Data Services on the Carte server by executing this endpoint in the Carte instance: `http://localhost:8082/kettle/listServices/`.

There's more...

At the moment, we are working with jobs and transformations that are stored and executed directly from our filesystem. However, it is possible to save and execute jobs and transformations from centralized Kettle repositories as well. The following repository types are available for us:

- **DI repository**: This is a repository that is available only on Pentaho Enterprise Edition, and is based on the Java Content Repository (JCR), which provides version control and referential integrity checks.

- **Kettle database repository**: This database repository is used to save jobs and transformations in a relational database. You can generate this repository from the Spoon user interface.

- **Kettle file repository**: This is the simplest of the repositories and is based on any kind of folder in the filesystem.

Running the Pentaho Data Integration server in a single instance

This recipe guides you through starting a Data Integration server and the simple steps required to work with a Data Integration repository. We will add a MongoDB MapReduce transformation to the DI repository and define a data service that runs from the server.

Getting ready

To get ready for this recipe, you first need to start the MongoDB server with the same database as that of the last chapter. You will also have to verify that `<user home folder>/.pentaho/metastore` is accessible to Data Integration server.

How to do it...

To run the DI Server, perform the following steps:

1. There is a `ctlscript.sh` script for Unix/Linux operating systems and **ctlscript.bat** for Windows operating systems in the Pentaho EE suite. This allows you to control the servers packed in the platform. We can start, stop, and restart various servers using this script:

    1. Open a command-line tool on your operating system and navigate to the `<pentaho-installation-path>/` folder.

    2. Execute the `./ctlscript.sh help` command to get all the available options for managing the Pentaho suite.

    3. Next, execute the `./ctlscript.sh start` command and all Pentaho services will start. As we mentioned before, it is possible to execute various servers manually using this script. We could have run the postgres server first (needed for the data integration server) and the Data Integration server afterwards using `./ctlscript.sh start postgresql` and then `./ctlscript.sh start data-integration-server`.

2. Another way of running the DI server is by executing the `<pentaho-installation-path>/server/data-integration-server/start-pentaho.sh` file for Unix/Linux operating systems and `<pentaho-installation-path>/server/data-integration-server/start-pentaho.bat` for Windows operating systems. Even in Windows, you can start the DI server from the **Start** menu by going to **Start | Pentaho Enterprise Edition | Server Management | Start Data Integration Server**.

3. Check whether or not the DI server has started correctly by accessing `http://localhost:9080/pentaho-di` in your web browser. You should get a login page similar to what is shown in this screenshot:

1. You should see a login screen. Enter `admin` as the username and `password` as the password.

2. You can list the available Kettle Data Services by navigating to the `http://localhost:9080/pentaho-di/kettle/listServices` endpoint.

4. Open the `chapter1-mongodb-map-reduce-writelog-without-parameter.ktr` file in Spoon, save it as `chapter2-mongodb-map-reduce.ktr`, and change the transformation name to `MongoDB MapReduce Kettle Thin`.

5. Save the transformation in the DI repository.

1. In the main menu, navigate to **Tools | Repository** and click on **Connect...** or press *Ctrl + R*.

2. Click on the plus icon to add a new repository.

3. Once the **Select the repository type** opened, select the **DI Repository** option. The following screenshot is seen:

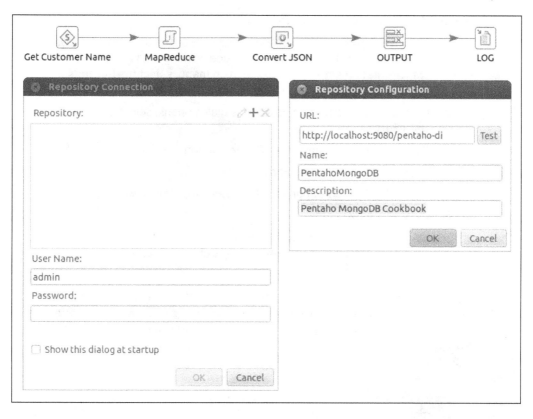

Get Customer Name   MapReduce   Convert JSON   OUTPUT   LOG

4. In the Repository configuration dialog, enter `http://localhost:9080/pentaho-di` in the **URL** property, `PentahoMongoDB` in the **Name** property, and `Pentaho MongoDB Cookbook` for the **Description** property. Then click on the **OK** button.

5. In the **Repository Connection** dialog, use the default credentials; the username is **admin** and the password is **password**. Click on **OK**. Then, in the **Close files** dialog, click on the **No** button.

6. Saving your transformation will display the **Transformation properties** dialog. Click on **OK** and then the **Enter comment** dialog will appear with a default comment. Click on **OK** again. The comments dialog appears, because the Data Integration Repository is based on the JRC version control.

6. Define a data service for this transformation.

    1. Open the **Transformation settings** dialog by any of these ways: press *Ctrl + T*; right-click on the right-hand side working area and select **Transformation settings**; or in the main menu, select the **Settings...** item entry from the **Edit** menu.

    2. Once the **Transformation properties** dialog opens, select the **Data Service** tab.

    3. Click on the **Create new Data Service** button.

    4. Set the new virtual table property to `MapReduceTable`.

    5. Select the **OUTPUT** option of the **Service step** drop-down property.

    6. Click on the **OK** button.

    7. Save the transformation again. Because you are connected to the DI repository, the **Enter comment** dialog is displayed. Enter a comment and click on **OK**.

7. Register the new `PentahoMongoDB` repository with the DI server by adding the following XML to the `<pentaho-ee-installation-path>/server/data-integration-server/pentaho-solutions/system/kettle/slave-server-config.xml` file inside the `slave_config` tag:

   ```
   <slave_config>
     ...
     <repository>
       <name>PentahoMongoDB</name>
       <username>admin</username>
       <password>password</password>
     </repository>
   </slave_config>
   ```

8. The MongoDB driver is not available in the full class path of the DI server, and it is necessary to add it. Copy the MongoDB driver from `<pentaho-ee-installation-path>/design-tools/data-integration/plugins/pentaho-mongodb-plugin/lib/mongo-java-driver-2.13.0.jar` and paste it in the `<pentaho-ee-installation-path>/server/data-integration-server/tomcat/webapps/pentaho-di/WEB-INF/lib` folder.

9. Restart the Data Integration server using the `./ctlscript.sh restart data-integration-server` command.

10. Get the `MapReduceTable` service definition by navigating to the `http://localhost:9080/pentaho-di/kettle/listServices` endpoint.

For Windows operating systems, if you don't see your service, one of the reasons is that you probably have the wrong value for the KETTLE_HOME variable.

KETTLE_HOME is the home folder of the .kettle folder. Inside the latter, you can find configurations for Pentaho Data Integration, for example, the repositories.xml file. As the DI Server is running as a service over the Administrator user, the KETTLE_HOME variable has the C:\ value by default.

> ▶ There are two things that you can do to fix this:
>
> ▶ Copy the repositories.xml file from your home user; for example, copy it from C:\Users\<user home folder>\.kettle\repositories.xml to C:\.kettle\repositories.xml.
>
> ▶ Stop the DI server service and run the following command from <pentaho-installation-path>/server/data-integration-server/tomcat/bin:

```
tomcat6.exe //US//pentahoDataIntegrationServer
++JvmOptions -DKETTLE_HOME=C:\Users\<user home
folder>\.kettle\repositories.xml
```

How it works...

The user interface of the DI server looks similar to the Carte server. However, Carte is a lightweight web server based on the Jetty server and doesn't provide enterprise features, such as scheduling jobs or transformations. The DI server is a Tomcat-based server with more capabilities for integration systems, for example, LDAP authentication.

In this recipe, we walked you through the steps for managing the DI server using the ctlscript.sh script. It's worth noting that it is also possible to use the start-pentaho and stop-pentaho scripts from the <pentaho-ee-installation-path>/server/data-integration-server/ folder.

Define a connection using a SQL Client (SQuirreL SQL)

In this recipe, we will guide you through the steps required to connect to your MongoDB instance via the JDBC-based SQuirreL SQL Client. We will be using the Thin Kettle JDBC Driver to make the connection to the MongoDB instance.

The SQuirreL SQL Client is a SQL client open source project, and it is possible to connect to any database that provides a JDBC driver, such as Thin Kettle.

Getting ready

To get ready for this recipe, you first need to start the MongoDB server with the same database as that of the last chapter. Then make sure that the Carte and DI servers are running. Download SQL Squirrel from `http://squirrel-sql.sourceforge.net` and install it in your computer by following the instructions on the website.

How to do it ...

Once we have our Carte or DI Server up and running, we can configure a SQL client to fire some SQL queries and get some data back. Perform the following steps to configure a Squirrel SQL client:

1. Open your Squirrel SQL Client.
2. Define a new JDBC driver. To do this, you can perform the following steps:
    1. Click on the **Drivers** tab from left side of Squirrel SQL Client.
    2. Click on the button with the plus icon; or in the tools menu, click on **Drivers** and then on **New Driver....** You will see an **Add Driver** dialog. This will allow you to define the Java Class Path and the Driver name on your Squirrel SQL Client.
    3. Set the **Name** property to `Kettle Thin`.
    4. Set **Example URL** to `jdbc:pdi://<server:port>/ kettle?<option=value>`.
    5. Select the **Extra Class Path** tab. Click on the **Add** button and add the following .jar files from your `<pentaho-installation-path>/ design-tools/data-integration/lib` folder:
        - `kettle-core-<version>.jar`
        - `kettle-engine-<version>.jar`
        - `commons-httpclient-3.1.jar`
        - `commons-codec-1.5.jar`
        - `commons-lang-2.6.jar`
        - `commons-logging-1.1.1.jar`
        - `commons-vfs-<version>-pentaho.jar`
        - `log4j-1.2.16.jar`
        - `scannotation-1.0.2.jar`
    6. Click on the **List Drivers** button.

7. Select the **org.pentaho.di.core.jdbc.ThinDriver** option for the **Class Name** property. Your setup should look similar to the following screenshot:

8. Click on the **OK** button to save the driver configuration.

3. Configure the connection for the Carte server. To do this, perform the following steps:

   1. Select the **Aliases** tab from left side of Squirrel SQL Client.

   2. Click on the button with a plus icon; or in the tools menu, click on **Aliases** and then on **New Alias...**.

   3. Once the **Add Alias** dialog opens, set the **Name** property to Pentaho Carte Server Conn.

   4. Select the In the **Driver** property, select **Kettle Thin** option.

   5. For the **URL** property, change the connection text to jdbc:pdi:// localhost:8082/kettle.

   6. The default **User Name** and **Password** properties are both cluster.

   7. Click on the **Test** button to test the connection, and you should see the **Connection successful** dialog. Your setup should look similar to what is shown in the following screenshot:

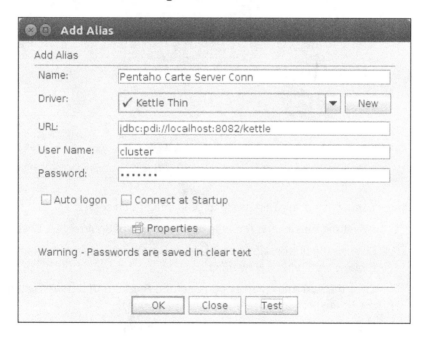

8. Click on the **OK** button to save the connection configuration.

With the connection defined, you can now connect to Carte using your Thin Kettle connection. Double-click on the **Pentaho Carte Server Conn** connection and click on the **Connect** button. You will have a new session tab opened, as shown in the following screenshot. In this session, you can execute basic operations such as running SQL queries, listing tables, and listing columns of a particular table.

1. Run SQL queries:

    1. Select the **SQL** tab in the **Pentaho Carte Server Conn** session.

    2. Write `select * from AggregationTable`, in the text area.

    3. Execute the SQL query by any of these ways: click on **Run SQL** button; in the tools menu, select **Session** and then click on **Run SQL**, or just press *Ctrl + Enter*. You will get the query result as shown in the following screenshot:

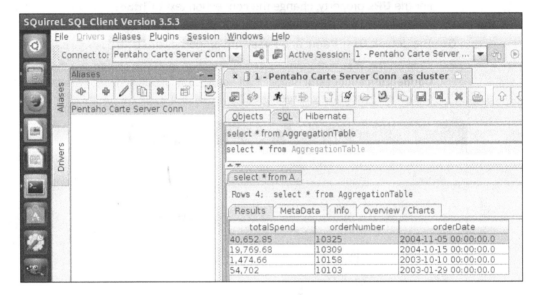

2. Define a connection using Thin Kettle to Data Integration server:

    1. Select the **Aliases** tab from the left-hand side of Squirrel SQL Client.

    2. Click on the button with a plus icon. Alternatively, in the tools menu, click on **Aliases** and then on **New Alias...**.

    3. Once the **Add Alias** dialog opens, set the **Pentaho DI Server Conn** name for the **Name** property.

    4. In the **Driver** property, select the **Kettle Thin** option.

    5. Set the **URL** property to **jdbc:pdi://localhost:9080/kettle?webappname=pentaho-di**.

6. The default **User Name** and **Password** properties are admin and password, respectively.

7. Click on the **Test** button to test the connection, and you should get a **Connection successful** dialog. The connection configuration should be similar to what is shown in the following screenshot:

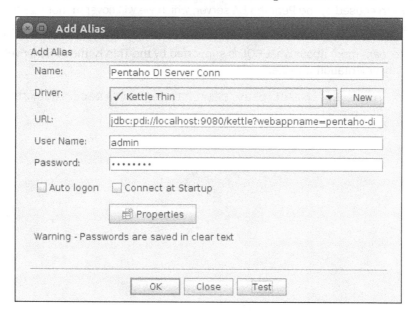

8. Click on the **OK** button to save the connection configuration.

3. With the connection defined, we are able to execute SQL queries against the connection. The steps are exactly the same as executing queries on the Carte server, the only difference being that you are running them on the DI Server.

How it works...

The driver is registered in SQuirreL using a set of Java libraries. The kettle-core-<version>.jar file is the main library that is used to create the connection, and it contains the org.pentaho.di.core.jdbc.ThinDriver class. The other .jar files are dependencies of the kettle library. These Java libraries are required to make the connection to the Carte or DI server and execute the SQL queries that we described before. Think of the Carte or DI Server as the "Kettle Database."

This recipe uses the Squirrel SQL Client as an example. However, you can use some other SQL client and develop a solution using this JDBC or using any reporting solution that is JDBC-based.

There's more...

The Thin Kettle JDBC Driver is limited to only performing select queries. It does not have the ability to execute inserts, updates, deletes, and so on. With the `select` ability, we can support connections to Mondrian. Mondrian is a ROLAP (short for Relational Online Analytical Processing) server used by the Pentaho BA server, which we will cover in more detail in the next couple of chapters.

If you want to learn more about what SQL is supported by the Thin Kettle JDBC Driver, you can consult this documentation website:

```
http://wiki.pentaho.com/display/EAI/JDBC+and+SQL+Reference#JDBCandSQL
Reference-SQLSupport
```

3
Pentaho Instaview

In this chapter, we will cover the following recipes:

- ▸ Creating an analysis view
- ▸ Modifying Instaview transformations
- ▸ Modifying the Instaview model
- ▸ Exploring, saving, deleting, and opening analysis reports

Introduction

Pentaho Instaview is a plugin for Pentaho data integration and is available in the Enterprise Edition version only. This plugin is designed for the user to instantly parse, model, and analyze data from different data sources, such as MongoDB.

Creating an analysis view

This recipe guides you through the process of parsing and profiling from a MongoDB collection and creating an instant analysis report.

Getting ready

To get ready for this recipe, you first need to start Spoon and the MongoDB server with the same database as that of the previous chapter.

How to do it...

Perform the following steps to create a simple analysis view:

1. In Spoon, change the perspective to **Instaview**. If you are using Windows operation the Windows operating system, you can start Instaview from the Start menu by selecting **Pentaho Enterprise Edition | Design Tools | Instaview**.

2. Click on the **Create New** button.

3. In the **New Data Source** dialog, select the **Big Data** tab. Next, select **MongoDB** and click on **OK**.

4. Define the MongoDB connection by performing the following steps:

    1. In the MongoDB input, select **Configure Connection** tab.

    2. Set the host name(s) or IP address(es) to **localhost**.

    3. Set **Port** to the default port number, which is **27017**.

    4. Select the **Input options** tab.

    5. Click on the **Get DBs** button and select the **SteelWheels** option for the **Database** field. Click on **Get collections** and select the **Orders** option for the **Collection** field.

    6. Select the **Fields** tab.

    7. Uncheck the **Output single JSON field** option;

    8. Click on the **Get fields** button. After analyzing the sample documents, remove the **_id** field from the list. You should get the list as shown in the following screenshot:

#	Name	Path	Type	Indexed values	Sample: array min:max index	Sample: #occur/#docs
1	customerNumber	S.customer.customerNumber	Integer			100/100
2	code	S.product.code	String			100/100
3	totalPrice	S.totalPrice	Number			100/100
4	requiredDate	S.requiredDate	Date			100/100
5	orderDate	S.orderDate	Date			100/100
6	orderLineNumber	S.orderLineNumber	Integer			100/100
7	time	S.customer.time	Date			100/100
8	priceEach	S.priceEach	Number			100/100
9	shippedDate	S.shippedDate	Date			100/100
10	orderNumber	S.orderNumber	Integer			100/100
11	quantityOrdered	S.quantityOrdered	Integer			100/100
12	status	S.status	String			100/100

9. Click on **OK**.

5. After the data of the connection has been processed, you should see the interactive analytics screen as shown in the following screenshot:

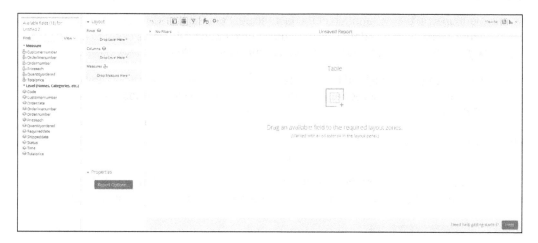

6. Drag and drop the **Totalprice** measure into the **Measures** area. You'll get the global number of the total price.

7. Drag and drop the **Orderdate** level into the **Rows** area. Instantly, you'll get the total price by order date.

8. Click on the **Save view** button.

9. Next, click on the **Close** button, and in the **Save Datasource** dialog, set **MongoDB Orders** to the data source name and click on the **Save** button.

How it works...

Pentaho Instaview is based on three main simple steps: choose the data source, auto-prepare the data for analysis, and Pentaho interactive visualize and explore. This recipe demonstrates all of them. However, as in any self-service or automated solution, sometimes it is necessary to customize and optimize the solution. The next recipe is about the modifications that you can make in Pentaho Instaview.

After the first step, choosing the data source (MongoDB, in this case), we define the connection to our collection for the second step. As you probably noticed, the interface for defining the connection looks similar to Spoon. This is because Pentaho Instaview creates a transformation to be executed in order to make the data available for exploring and visualizing. In the next recipe, we will demonstrate how you can edit this transformation.

The end result is an interactive visualization report that allows you to explore your data quickly. However, the metadata model that was generated automatically is a little inaccurate. Nevertheless, it's possible to change it, as is explained in one of the later recipes.

Modifying Instaview transformations

As was mentioned in the explanation of the last recipe, Pentaho Instaview automatically creates ETL transformations to define data flow from the source (MongoDB in this case) to the target. Instaview gives us the ability to edit those transformations with Pentaho data integration.

This recipe guides you through editing the transformation of MongoDB Orders data source, which was created in the last recipe, in order to get better and cleaner data from the MongoDB database.

Getting ready

To get ready for this recipe, you first need to start Instaview with the **MongoDB Orders** data source, and the MongoDB server with the same database as that of the last chapter.

How to do it...

As with any automated tool there is always something that needs to be tweaked. Perform the following steps to make a little change to the transformation that populates data into the analysis view:

1. In **Instaview** home, click on the **Open Existing** button.

2. Select **MongoDB Orders** from the **Data Sources** list and click on **OK**.

3. Click on the **Configure** tab.

4. Next, click on the **Edit** link of **Data Integration** section. Accept the alert about editing the transformation by clicking on the **OK** button.

5. Add the order year and month to the transformation as follows:

    1. Select the **Design** tab in the left-hand-side view of the **Data Integration** perspective.

    2. From the **Transform category** folder, find the **Calculator** step and drag and drop it into the working area in the right-hand-side view.

    3. Connect the **Input** step to the new **Calculator** step and then connect the **Calculator** step to the **Do Not Edit** step.

    4. Double-click on the **Calculator** step to open the configuration dialog.

    5. Add a new field by clicking on **New field** and name it `orderYearDate` as the calculation is **Year of date A**, and select **orderDate** in the column **Field A**.

6. Again, add a new field named `orderMonthDate` as the calculation is **Month of date A**, and select **orderDate** in the column **Field A**.

7. Click on the **OK** button of the **Calculator** step and save the transformation. The transformation structure should be like that shown in the following screenshot:

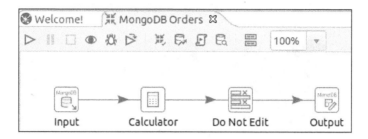

6. Save the transformation and change to the **Instaview** perspective.

7. Click on the **Run** button as seen in the following screenshot:

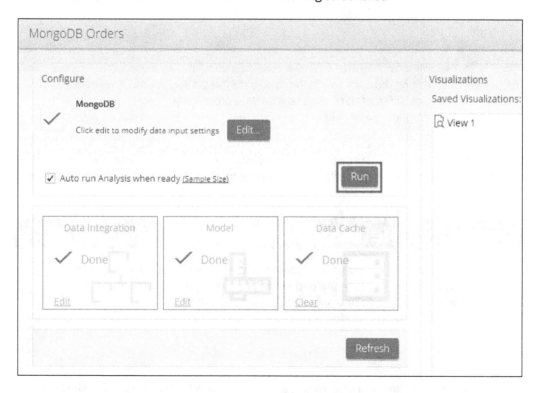

8. After the execution, the two new levels will be visible in the report. Drag and drop the **orderYearDate** level into the **Rows** area, **orderMonthDate** into the **Columns** area, and then drag and drop **Totalprice** into the **Measures** area. Basically, you have a report with the total price of order by year over each month, as shown in the following screenshot:

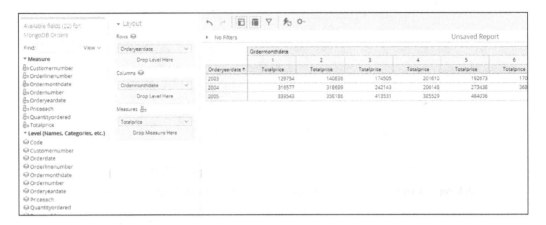

How it works...

The possibility of editing the data flow in Pentaho data integration opens many doors to solutions that require different data sources and data processing. In this recipe, we just changed the transformation a little to add two new fields useful for analysis reporting.

Basically, we change the transformation responsible for extracting the data for the report analysis. This allows us to aggregate the data in years and months. This was possible using the simple calculator step, which extracts the year or month from a specific date field in the data stream.

Modifying the Instaview model

As you have probably noticed, Pentaho Instaview automatically generates, based on our data, a metadata model. However, the end result in the analysis-reporting tool isn't easy to understand as the dimensions and measures have technical names. This recipe guides us through editing the metadata model.

Getting ready

To get ready for this recipe, you first need to start Instaview with the **MongoDB Orders** data source created and modified in previous recipes, and the MongoDB server with the same database as that of the last chapter.

How to do it...

Perform the following steps to edit the **Instaview** model:

1. In the **Instaview** home, click on the **Open Existing** button.

2. Select **MongoDB Orders** from the **Data Sources** list and click on **OK**.

3. Click on the **Configure** tab.

4. Next, click on the **Edit** link of the **Model** section. Accept the alert about model editing, by clicking on the **OK** button. You'll be redirected to the **Model Editor** perspective, as shown in the following screenshot:

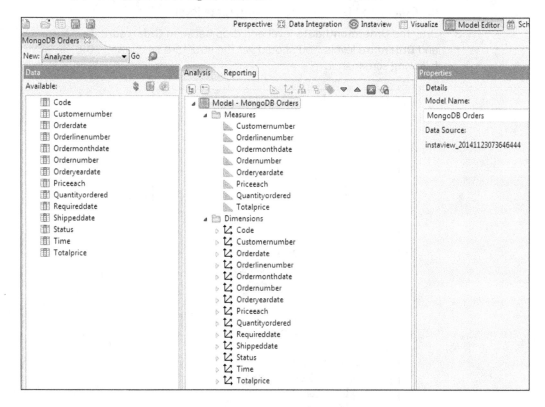

5. Remove the measures that don't make sense in the model. Select the **Customernumber** field and click on the red square button with the white **X** on the top. Do the same for the following fields: **Orderlinenumber**, **Ordermonthdate**, **Ordernumber**, and **Orderyeardate**.

6. Rename the measures to appropriate names. Select **Priceeach** and in the properties in the right-hand side, change **Display Name** to **Price Each**. Do the same for the following measures: **Quantityordered** to **Quantity Ordered** and **Totalprice** to **Total Price**.

7. Remove the dimensions that they are measuring in the model. Select the **Priceeach** field and click on the red button with the white **X**. Do the same for the following dimensions: **Quantityordered** and **Totalprice**.

8. Define the hierarchy of **Order Date** as follows:

   1. In the **Dimensions** tree expand the full tree of **Orderdate, Orderyeardate**, and **Ordermonthdate**.

   2. Drag the **Orderyeardate** level that has a yellow icon and drop it between the **Orderdate** hierarchy and the **Orderdate** level.

   3. Drag the **Ordermonthdate** level and drop between **Orderyeardate** and **Orderdate** levels. You should get the structure as shown in the following screenshot:

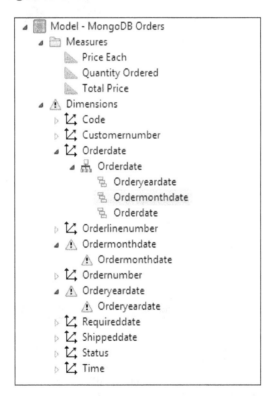

   4. Remove the useless dimensions, such as **Ordermonthdate** and **Orderyeardate**; they have a yellow exclamation icon.

9. Rename the dimension, hierarchies and levels as seen in the following screenshot:

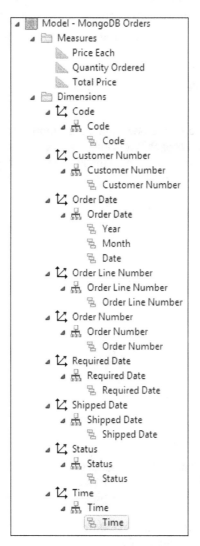

10. Define the dimension time by performing the following set of steps:

    1. Select the **Order Date** dimension and check the **Time Dimension** property.

    2. Then, select the **Year** level and the **Years** option of **Time Level** Type.

    3. Select the **Month** level and the **Months** option of **Time Level Type**.

    4. Next, select the **Date** level and the **Days** option of **Time Level Type**.

    5. Select the **Required Date** dimension and check the **Time Dimension** property.

6. Then, select the **Required Date** level and the **Days** option of **Time Level Type**.

7. Select the **Shipped Date** dimension and check the **Time Dimension** property.

8. Finally, select the **Shipped Date** level and the **Days** option of **Time Level Type**.

11. Save the analysis model by clicking on the **Save** button or by pressing *Ctrl + S*.

12. Change to the **Instaview** perspective.

13. Click on the **Run** button.

14. After the execution, you'll see new, and better, names for exploring your data. Drag and drop the **Year** and **Month** levels into the **Rows** area. Then, drag and drop the **Status** level into the **Columns** area. Finally, drag and drop the **Total Price** measure into the **Measures** area. You should get a report like this:

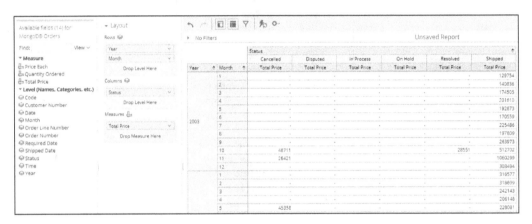

How it works...

In this recipe, we started by removing the measures that don't make sense existing. Basically, Pentaho Instaview defines any numeric column as a measure and all columns as dimensions. After this change, we rename the measure to be accurate with the data that we will analyze.

After we have clarified the measures (as we did the same for dimensions), we will start by removing dimensions that aren't necessary.

As with any OLAP solution, the date dimension is common. That's why we define the date dimension with the right hierarchy of years, months, and days.

Finally, we rename all dimensions and sub-attributes (hierarchies and levels). The end result is that the exploration data is clearer to understand.

See also

In *Chapter 4, A MongoDB OLAP Schema*, you can find out how to create a Mondrian schema.

Exploring, saving, deleting, and opening analysis reports

This recipe guides you through exploring, saving, deleting, and opening analysis reports in Instaview. These are the basic actions that can be done in Instaview, as the goal of Instaview is to quickly explore data. These actions are simple for end users.

Getting ready

To get ready for this recipe, you first need to start Instaview with the **MongoDB Orders** data source, created and modified in previous recipes, and the MongoDB server with the same database as that of the last chapter.

How to do it...

To understand how to use Instaview, perform the following steps:

1. In **Instaview** home, click on the **Open Existing** button.
2. Select **MongoDB Orders** from the **Data Sources** list and click on **OK**.
3. Click on the **Configure** tab and then on the **Run** button.
4. After the execution is complete, open the analyzer, and let's explore the data:
   1. Drag and drop the **Year** and **Month** levels into the **Rows** area. Then drag and drop the **Status** level into the **Columns** area. Finally, drag and drop the **Total Price** and **Quantity Ordered** measures into the **Measures** area.

2. We will be filtering the data for the year 2003 by clicking on the year arrow, selecting **Filter...**, and then selecting the **2003** option. The **Include** list after adding the year is shown in this screenshot:

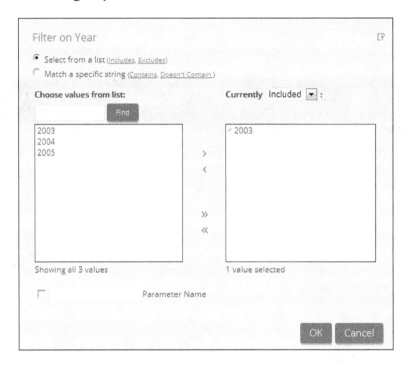

3. Click on the **OK** button of the **Filter on Year** dialog.

4. Change the view to a chart by clicking on the chart icon of **View As**, and select the **Stacked Column** option. You should get a chart like that shown in the following screenshot:

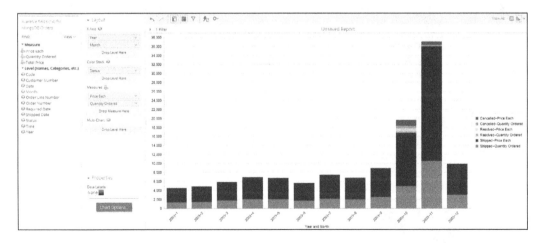

5. Click on **Save View** to save your visualization.

6. Click on the **Configure** tab, and you will get a list of the views that you saved before for opening again, as shown in this screenshot:

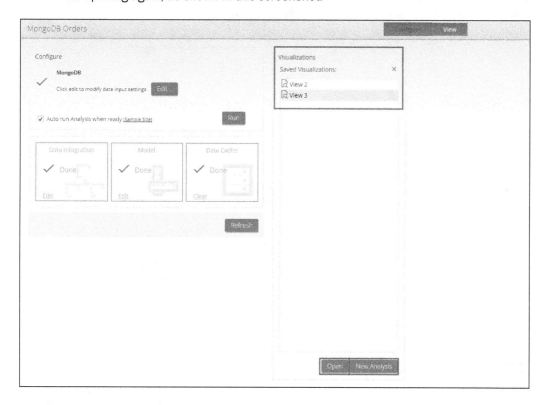

How it works...

This recipe covered the main functionalities for exploring, saving, deleting, and managing your analysis with Pentaho Instaview.

Analysis Reporting or Pentaho Analyzer (a Pentaho BI server plugin) is a drag-and-drop solution that allows the user to explore your data with ease. We started this recipe by creating a simple view that showed the total price and the quantity ordered, aggregated by months for different status. Then, we filtered the data for the year 2003 and changed the visualization from a table to a stacked column chart.

This Analysis-Reporting tool supports different visualization types, such as tables, geomaps, and charts with the possibility of exporting in different file types.

See also

In *Chapter 6, The Pentaho BI Server*, which is about the Pentaho BI server, you can find more information about the Pentaho Analyzer plugin.

4

A MongoDB OLAP Schema

In this chapter, we will cover these recipes:

- ▸ Creating a date dimension
- ▸ Creating an Orders cube
- ▸ Creating the customer and product dimensions
- ▸ Saving and publishing a Mondrian schema
- ▸ Creating a Mondrian 4 physical schema
- ▸ Creating a Mondrian 4 cube
- ▸ Publishing a Mondrian 4 schema

Introduction

In this chapter, you'll learn how to create **OLAP** (short for **Online Analytical Processing**) schemas for Pentaho with MongoDB as a data source. OLAP is an approach to creating multidimensional analyses. Pentaho uses the **ROLAP** (short for **Relational Online Analytical Processing**) engine, called by **Mondrian** to convert **MDX** (short for **Multidimensional Expressions**) queries into SQL queries.

If you aren't a business intelligence consultant, you probably have never heard about **data warehouse** and the preceding terms. Essentially, a data warehouse is a system for storing historical data from different data sources, so that you're prepared to use reporting systems, for example, Pentaho and Mondrian. This is a quick and simple explanation, but it is recommended that you carry out research about these terms, as this book is focused on using Pentaho and MongoDB, and not business intelligence technologies.

As Mondrian is responsible for generating SQL queries and MongoDB does not support it, it's necessary that we use a layer to convert SQL to MongoDB queries. With Pentaho, there are three main ways to create OLAP using MongoDB. Based on your requirements or customer requirements, you should choose one of these:

▸ **RDBMS**: Use a relational database, in preference to a column-oriented database, and connect Mondrian on top. You need to create an ETL to get the data from MongoDB and load it into the relational database. This is the approach that was used long before NoSQL databases became popular.

▸ **Thin Kettle JDBC Driver**: This approach uses Pentaho Data Integration as the layer responsible for getting the MongoDB data, based on an SQL query. Depending on the hardware and the configurations, it is possible that you will face performance issues with a lot of data in MongoDB. This approach is only possible with Pentaho Enterprise Edition because the Thin Kettle JDBC Driver is available on that version only.

▸ **Mondrian 4 and Pentaho EE native connector for MongoDB**: The latest version of Pentaho Enterprise Edition comes with Mondrian 4 and a connector for MongoDB. This is probably the best approach based on performance—using MongoDB and Mondrian. However, this native connection works for single collections only. This means that you need all of the data for about one fact in a single JSON document, because the current MongoDB versions doesn't support joins.

In summary, this chapter is divided into two main parts. One is about creating a regular cube using the Thin Kettle JDBC Driver and Mondrian 3.x. We'll use two transformations that come in the source code of this chapter as our Thin Kettle JDBC data services: `chapter4-getdates` and `chapter4-getorders`. As was explained in previous chapters, you should be able to convert those transformations into data services. It is possible, in a particular way, to use this part to create a Mondrian schema for RDBMS, just by changing the database connection.

The second part is about the new Mondrian 4.x schema. This is done using the native connection for MongoDB, which is available on Pentaho Enterprise Edition only.

Creating a date dimension

In this recipe, we guide you to start creating a Mondrian 3.x schema with the **Schema Workbench**, using the Thin Kettle JDBC Driver as the connection. We'll first create a shared dimension, **date**. A shared dimension can be referenced in different cubes. However, in this particular case, it is not necessary to have a shared dimension because we'll have just one cube.

Getting ready

Before you start this recipe, you need to make sure that the MongoDB server is running with the databases created in the previous chapters, and that the Data Integration server is running.

How to do it...

Proceed with the following steps:

1. Open the **Schema Workbench** application. On Windows, you can find it in the **Start** menu. From there, go to **Pentaho Enterprise Edition | Design Tools | Schema Workbench**. On Linux, you need to run a command like this:

   ```
   sh <pentaho-installation-path>/design-tools/
   schema-workbench/workbench.sh
   ```

2. With the **Schema Workbench** opened, let's configure the database connection. In this case, it will be the Data Integration server:

   1. In the main menu, select **Options** and then **Connection...**.

   2. In the **Database Connection** popup, you have to define a connection name as **Pentaho MongoDB Cookbook**. Select the **Kettle thin JDBC driver** option for **Connection Type**. The **Host Name** parameter is **localhost**, **Database Name** is **kettle?webappname=pentaho-di**, **Port Number** is **9080**, **User Name** is **admin**, and **Password** is **password**. Your setup should look similar to what is shown in this screenshot:

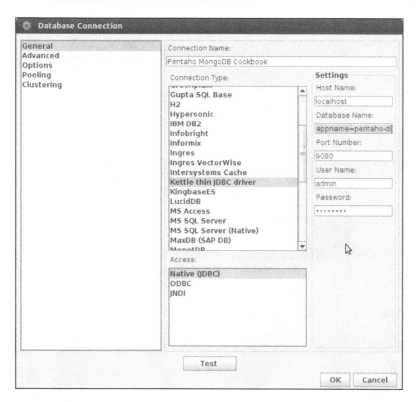

Click on the **Test** button and you should get a success message box. Then click on the **OK** button.

Let's start creating the OLAP schema properly:

1. In the main menu, go to **File | New | Schema**, and you should get a subwindow for creating the new schema, as you can see here:

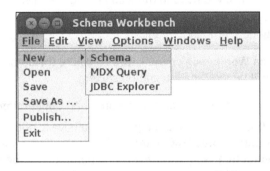

2. Select the **Schema** object and set **Orders** as the field name.

3. Right-click on the **Schema** object and select **Add Dimension**, as you can see in the following screenshot:

4. Add a table to the hierarchy by right-clicking and selecting **Add Table**, as you can see in this screenshot:

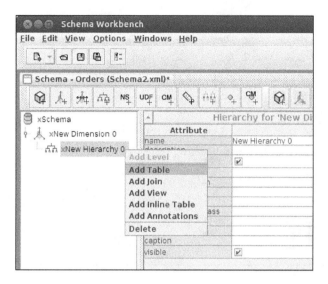

5. After selecting the table object added, select the **Kettle->date** option for the **name** field, as shown here:

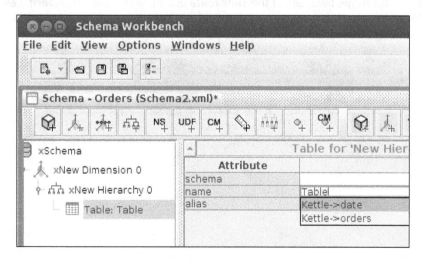

6. In the default hierarchy (`New Hierarchy 0`), right-click and select the **Add Level** option, as you can see in this screenshot:

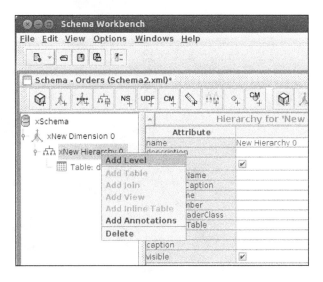

7. Let's define the year for this new level. Having selected the level object, set the **name** field to **year**. Select the option **year** from the **column** field and **String** in the **type** field. In the **levelType** field, select the **TimeYears** option, and in **hideMemberIf**, select the **Never** option. Finally, for the **caption** field, set **Year**. You can see all of these in the following screenshot:

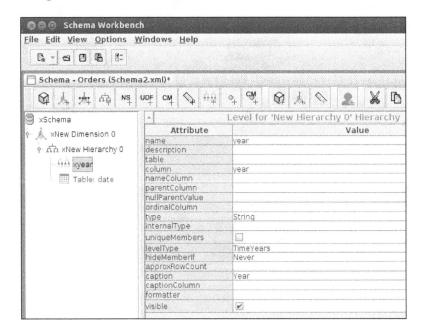

8. Add a new level and define the month, as shown here:

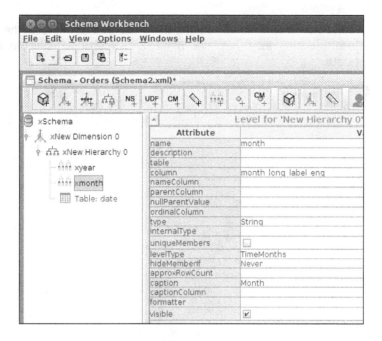

9. Next, add a new level and define the day, as you can see in the following screenshot:

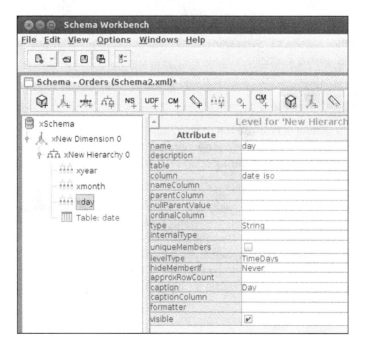

10. Select the hierarchy object, remove the default name (**New Hierarchy 0**), and select **date** for the **primaryKey** field.

11. Next, select the dimension object, and for the **name** field, set **date**. In the **type** field, select **TimeDimension**, as you can see in the next screenshot. Finally, in the **caption** field, set **Date**.

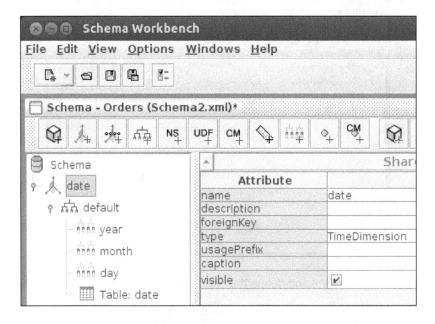

12. Select other objects that you want and you shouldn't see any more red alerts. Our date dimension is defined.

How it works...

We started with the **Schema Workbench**. It is an application that helps create a Mondrian schema. First, we created a database connection, in this case using the Kettle Thin JDBC Driver. This connection will help us during schema creation with red alert messages at the bottom of the screen.

Then, we created a simple date dimension in the schema with one hierarchy that contains three levels of granularity. With these three levels, when exploring the cube, we can aggregate our measures by year, month, or day. Basically, with some plugins, such as **Analysis Report** or **Saiku Analytics**, it's possible to explore—using a good drag-and-drop interface—the future **Orders** cube while aggregating the data by year, month, or day. In this way, you will get answers for questions such as "What is the total price for each year?" or "What is the quantity of products ordered in January 2013?".

There's more...

Here are some definitions for the main keywords related to the Mondrian schema:

- **Schema**: This defines a multidimensional logical model consisting of cubes, hierarchies, and members that help map the model onto the physical model

- **Cube**: This is a data structure that allows fast analysis of data according to the multiple dimensions that define a business problem

- **Dimension**: This is a set of hierarchies that provide information to otherwise unordered numeric measures

- **Hierarchy**: This is a logical tree structure that defines parent-child relationships in a dimension

- **Level**: This is a collection of members that have the same distance from the parent of the hierarchy

- **Member**: This is a point within a dimension determined by a particular set of attribute values

Creating an Orders cube

This recipe guides you through creating an **Orders** cube and linking the shared **Date** dimension to the business fact dates, such as **order date**, **required date**, and **shipped date**. We will be creating the main measures, such as the *total price*, the *quantity ordered*, and the *calculated measured average price*.

Getting ready

Before you start this recipe, you need to make sure that you have the MongoDB database created, as done in the previous chapters. The Data Integration server should be running and you should have the schema you created in the previous recipe.

How to do it...

Proceed with the following steps:

1. In the **Schema**, right-click on it and select the **Add Cube** option, or you can just click on the **Add Cube** icon in the tools menu of your subwindow.

2. Select the new cube object and set the **name** field to **Orders** and the **caption** field to **Orders**, as you can see here:

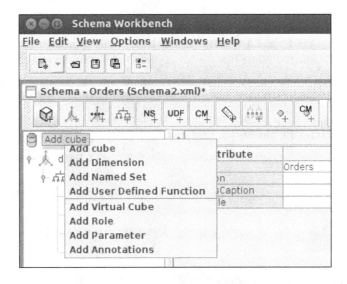

3. Select the **Orders** cube, right-click, and select **Add Table**. Next, select the table object, and for the **name** field, select the **Kettle->orders** option.

4. Let's add the relation of our **Date** dimension to the Orders cube. Right-click on the **Orders** cube and select **Add Dimension Usage**. In the new dimension usage object, set the **name** field to **orderDate**. For the **foreignKey** field, select the **orderDate** option; for the **source** field, select **date**; and for the **caption** field, set **Order date**. The configuration should be similar to the following screenshot:

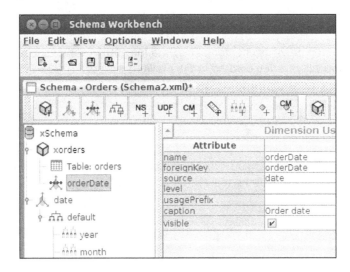

5. As you did in the step before, add a new dimension usage for the required date. The configuration should be similar to what is shown in this screenshot:

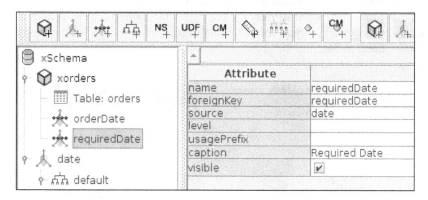

6. Again, as you did in the step before, add a new dimension usage for the shipped date. The configuration should be similar to the following:

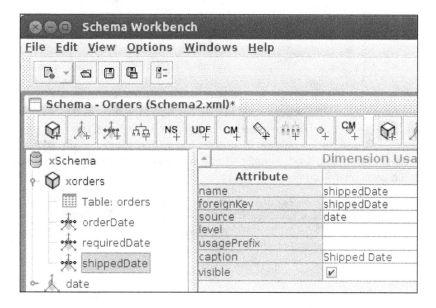

Let's add some measures to the Orders:

1. Right-click on the **Orders** cube and select **Add Measure**. In the new measure object, set the **name** field to **totalPrice**. For the **aggregator** field, select the **sum** option, and for the **column** field, select **totalPrice**. In **datatype**, select the **Numeric** option, and for the **caption** field, set **Total Price**. The configuration should be similar to what is shown in this screenshot:

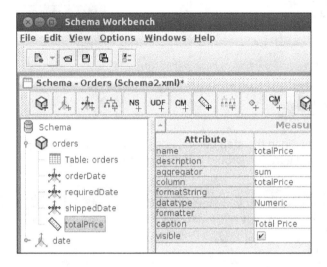

2. Now, right-click on the **Orders** cube and select **Add Measure**. In the new measure object, set the **name** field to **quantityOrdered**. For the **aggregator** field, select the **sum** option, and for the **column** field, select **quantityOrdered**. In **datatype**, select the **Numeric** option, and for the **caption** field, set **Quantity Ordered**. The configuration should be similar what is shown here:

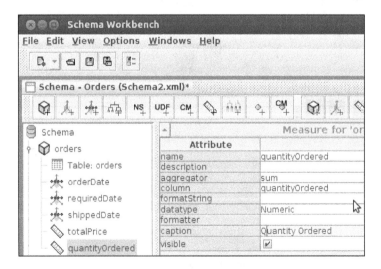

3. Next, right-click on the **Orders** cube and select **Add Calculated Member**. In the new calculated member object, set the **name** field to **avgPriceEach**. For the **caption** field, set **Avg Price Each**, and in the **formula** field, set `IIF([Measures].[totalPrice]=0,0,[Measures].[totalPrice]/[Measures].[quantityOrdered])`. The configuration should be similar to what is shown in the following screenshot:

How it works...

After creating the shared **Date** dimension, we create the proper **Orders** cube, where the Orders table is the physical fact table. In this case, it isn't a table but the Orders MongoDB collection. This cube has three date dimensions that link to the date-shared dimension. One dimension is for describing the date when the order was placed; it is the **Order Date** dimension. The next one is for describing by when the order was required; it is the **Required Date** dimension. And the last one is for describing when the order was shipped; it is the **Shipped Date** dimension.

This cube contains two measures and one calculated measure. One measure represents the total price of the products, which is the **Total Price** measure. Basically, it is a sum of the values in the **totalPrice** column in the **Orders** table. In other words, it is used to aggregate as a sum the values of the **totalPrice** property in the **Orders** collection. The other measure is the quantity of products ordered, which is the **Quantity Ordered** measure. Like the total price, this aggregates as a sum the values of the **quantityOrdered** property in the **Orders** collection.

The calculated measure value is then obtained by the division of **Total Price** by **Quantity Ordered**. In this way, we get the average price of each product ordered. As you can see, there exists a condition for checking whether the quantity ordered is zero. This is because sometimes, the ordered quantity can be zero. This verification exists because you can't divide a number by zero.

Creating the customer and product dimensions

In this recipe, we will guide you through creating degenerate customer and product dimensions. A degenerate dimension consists of a dimension that doesn't have its own physical table, and the data lives in the fact table. In other words, the customer and product JSON are sub-documents within the `Order` documents of the **Orders** MongoDB collection.

Getting ready

Before you start this recipe, you need to make sure you have the MongoDB databases created in previous chapters. Also, the Data Integration server should be running, and you will need the schema that you created in the previous recipe.

How to do it...

Proceed with the following steps:

1. Let's add the **Customer** dimension to the **Orders** cube:

    1. Right-click on the **Orders** cube and select **Add Dimension**.

    2. Expand the new dimension object, and in the default hierarchy created, remove the text for the **name** field. For the **primaryKey** field, select the **customerNumber** option.

3. Right-click on the hierarchy and select **Add Level**. Select the new level object and set the **name** field to **country**. Select the **customerCountry** option for the **column** field and the **String** option for the **type** field. In **levelType**, select the **Regular** option; in **hideMemberIf**, select the **Never** option; and finally for the **caption** field, set **Country**. The configuration should be similar to this:

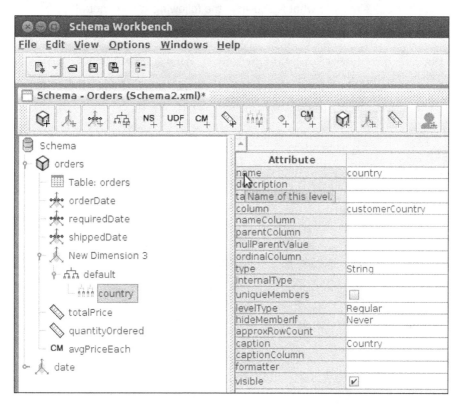

4. Again, right-click on the hierarchy and select **Add Level**. Select the new level object and set the **name** field to **name**. Then select the **customerName** option for the **column** field and the **String** option for the **type** field. In **levelType**, select the **Regular** option. In **hideMemberIf**, select the **Never** option, and for the **caption** field, set **Name**. Now, the configuration should look similar to what is shown in the following screenshot:

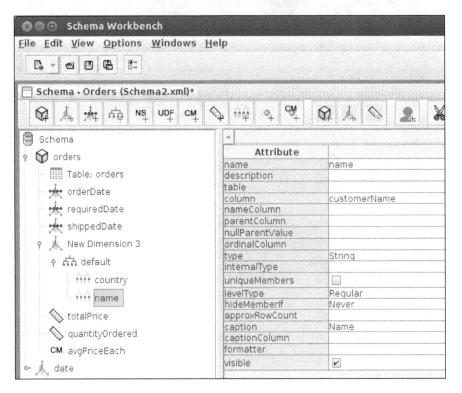

5. Select the dimension object and set the **name** field to **customer**. For **foreignKey**, select the **customerNumber** option, and in the **caption** field, set **Customer**. Thus, the configuration should be similar to what is shown here:

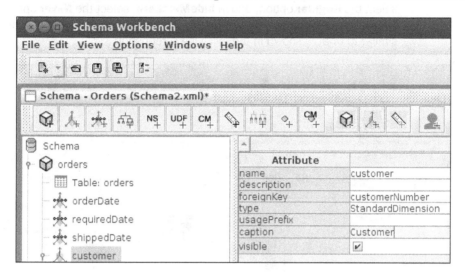

2. Let's now add the **Product** dimension to the **Orders** cube:

   1. Right-click on the **Orders** cube and select **Add Dimension**.

   2. Expand the new dimension object, and in the default hierarchy created, remove the text of the **name** field. For the **primaryKey** field, select the **productCode** option.

3. Right-click on the hierarchy and select **Add Level**. Next, select the new level object and set the **name** field to **name**. Then select the **productName** option for the **column** field and the **String** option for the **type** field. In **levelType**, select the **Regular** option, and in **hideMemberIf**, select the **Never** option. Finally, for the **caption** field, set **Name**. The configuration should now be similar to what is shown in the following screenshot:

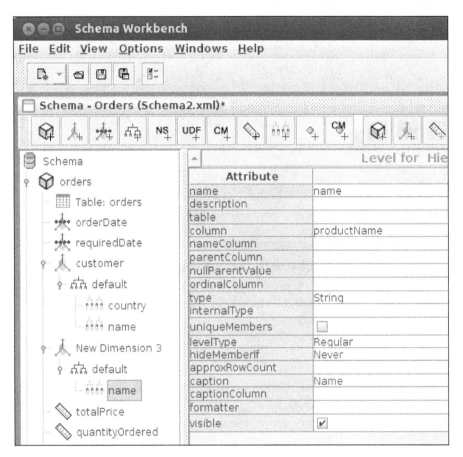

4. Select the dimension object and set the **name** field to **product**. For **foreignKey**, select the **productCode** option, and in the **caption** field, set **Product**. Thus, the configuration should be similar to this:

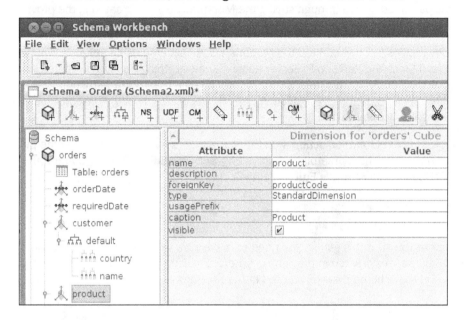

How it works...

In this recipe, we add two more dimensions: **product** and **customer**.

The customer dimension consists of one hierarchy with two levels; the first is the country and the second is the customer name. However, it could be possible to add more levels such as city and postal code, or create an address dimension with information about the address—the country, city, postal code, and detailed address.

The same is possible with the product dimension, which has just one level—the product name—and it's possible at a product line parent level. As the goal of this book is to explain how to work with Pentaho and MongoDB, we won't cover data warehousing modulation in too much detail.

See also

If you are looking to expand your knowledge about Mondrian schemas, you can check out the online documentation at `http://mondrian.pentaho.com/documentation/schema.php`.

Saving and publishing a Mondrian schema

In this recipe, we guide you through saving the Mondrian schema created in the previous recipes in the filesystem and publishing it on the Pentaho BI server.

In previous recipes, we just created the Mondrian OLAP schema using **Schema Workbench**, a desktop tool. Since the Pentaho BI server doesn't know anything about the created schema, it is necessary to publish it. This means that you will be able to perform particular BI operations after publishing it on the BI server, such as self-service analysis using **Pentaho Analyzer** and/or **Pentaho Dashboards**.

After publishing the Mondrian schema on the Pentaho BI server, you can use some plugins available in the Pentaho marketplace, such as **Ivy Schema Editor** (**IvySE**), **Community Text Editor** (**CTE**), **Pentaho Analysis Editor** (**PHASE**), and so on.

Getting ready

Again, before you start this recipe, you need to make sure you have these things: the MongoDB databases created in previous chapters, the Data Integration and BI servers running, and the schema that you created in the previous recipe.

How to do it...

Proceed with the following steps:

1. Let's save the schema in the filesystem. In the main menu, click on **File** and then on **Save**. Choose the location that you wish and set the filename to `KetteThin.mondrian.xml`.

2. Let's publish the schema on the Pentaho BI server:

   1. First, you need to make sure that you have the Pentaho BI server started. For example, you can run the `./ctlscript.sh start` main path command in your Pentaho installation for Linux systems. For Windows, click on the Start menu and select **Start Pentaho BI Server**. Another way in Windows is as follows: you start the Pentaho server services by going to **Control Panel | Administrative Tools | Services** and then start, stop, or restart the Pentaho service.

   2. After some minutes, you will be able to access the Pentaho BI server using the URL `http://localhost:8080/pentaho` for default installations.

   3. Enter your username and password; for example, the username can be **admin** and the password can be **password**.

4. After you have logged on, click on the **Manage Data Sources** button, as you can see in this screenshot:

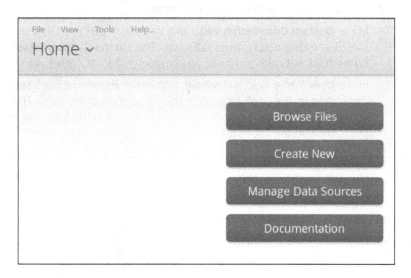

5. In the new **Manage Data Sources** dialog, click on the arrow and then select the **New Connection...** option, as you can see here:

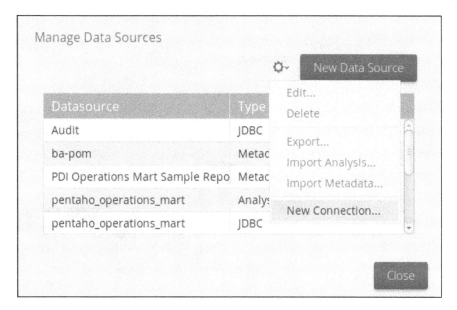

6. In the new **Database Connection** dialog, set `Pentaho MongoDB Cookbook Kettle Thin` for the **Connection Name** field. After this, set **Database Type** to **Generic database**.

7. In the **Custom Connection URL** field, set `jdbc:pdi://localhost:9080/kettle?webappname=pentaho-di`. Then in the **Custom Driver Class Name** field, set `org.pentaho.di.core.jdbc.ThinDriver`.

8. In the **User Name** field, set **admin**, and in the **Password** field, set **password**, depending on the configuration in the installation of Pentaho. The configuration should be similar to what is shown in the following screenshot. Then, click on the **OK** button.

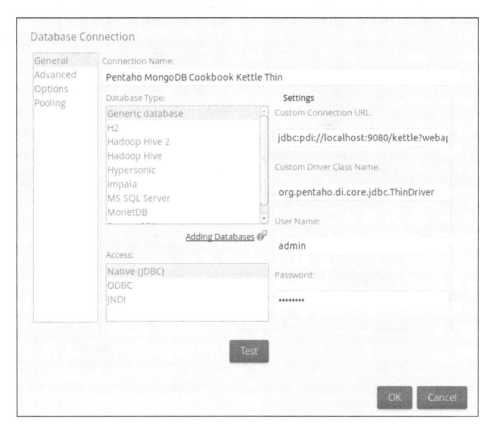

9. In the main menu of the **Schema Workbench**, select **File** and then select **Publish...**.

10. In the new **Publish Schema** dialog, set `http://localhost:8080/pentaho/` in the **Server URL** field. In the **User** field, set **admin**, and set **password** in the **Password** field, depending on the Pentaho installation. For the **Pentaho or JNDI Data Source** field, set **Pentaho MongoDB Cookbook Kettle Thin**. Then click on the **Publish** button. The configuration should be similar to this:

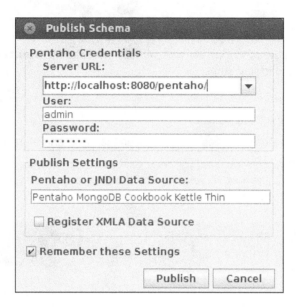

11. After a couple of seconds, we should get a message box with a **Publish Successful** message.

How it works...

In this recipe, we started by creating the database connection using the Kettle Thin JDBC driver in the Pentaho BI server. The connection is the same as that for the **Schema Workbench**, as the schema can simply work in the same connection. Otherwise, you face the risk of data being unavailable for exploration. This is because the schema is defined for a specific physical database structure.

Having defined the connection, we use the **Schema Workbench** to publish the Mondrian schema. Basically, we choose the server URL and the credentials for publishing (these were defined on the installation), and we define the connection name that will be used by the schema in the Pentaho BI server. Also, it is possible to make the schema available for **XMLA** (**XML for Analysis**).

XMLA is a standard for data access in analytical systems such as OLAP and data mining, based on standards such as XML, SOAP, and HTTP.

There's more...

It's possible to publish the Mondrian schema without the **Schema Workbench**. Basically, you need perform the following steps:

1. Log in to the Pentaho BI server.

2. Click on **Manage Data Sources**.

3. In the **Manage Data Sources** dialog, click on the arrow and then on **Import Analysis....**

4. In the **Import Analysis** dialog, you have to select the Mondrian schema in your filesystem. You also have to select the connection for the correct data source, as shown in the following screenshot:

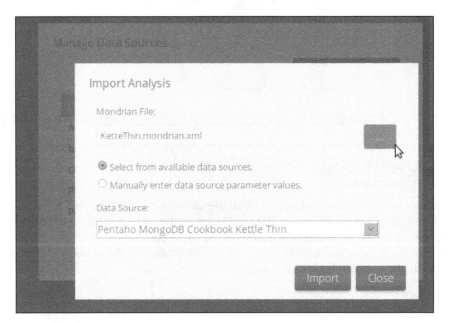

There are some interesting community plugins for handling the Mondrian schema, such as **Ivy Schema Editor** (**IvySE**) or **Pentaho Analysis Editor** (**PHASE**). You can check them out in the Pentaho marketplace.

Creating a Mondrian 4 physical schema

In this recipe, we will guide you so that you can start creating a Mondrian 4 schema for use with the MongoDB native connection. This feature is available only on Pentaho Enterprise Edition. In this particular recipe, we will start by creating the physical schema. This schema is responsible for defining the physical database. In this case, the data source, MongoDB, is where we specify the JSONPath of the fields in the collection.

As no GUI tool exists yet for managing this different OLAP schema, we'll use a normal text editor. However, there is a tool that helps to generate schemas automatically by editing Mondrian 4 schemas using MongoDB and managing the olap4j.properties file that is responsible for storing the connections information. You can get the source code on GitHub at https://github.com/kromerm/MondrianMongoModel.

Getting ready

Open your favorite text editor, such as Notepad, sublime text, or any other editor. We recommend a good one for XML syntax and indentation as the Mondrian schema is in XML.

How to do it...

Proceed with the following steps:

1. With the text editor opened, let's start by declaring the schema with the name Mondrian4MongoDBPentahoCookbook. We write this line:

   ```
   <Schema name='Mondrian4MongoDBPentahoCookbook'
   quoteSql='false' missingLink='ignore'
   metamodelVersion='4.00'></Schema>
   ```

2. Then let's add the **PhysicalSchema** tag to the **Schema** tag. Write the following line inside the **Schema** tag: `<PhysicalSchema></PhysicalSchema>`.

3. Add the **Orders** table (in this case, it is a collection, not a table) by writing this line inside the PhysicalSchema tag: `<Table name='Orders'></Table>`.

4. Finally, let's add the columns of the **Orders** collection by putting the following lines inside the **Table** tag:

```
<ColumnDefs>
  <CalculatedColumnDef name='orderDate' type='String'>
    <ExpressionView>
      <SQL dialect='generic'>
        $orderDate
      </SQL>
    </ExpressionView>
  </CalculatedColumnDef>
  <CalculatedColumnDef name='requiredDate' type='String'>
    <ExpressionView>
      <SQL dialect='generic'>
        $requiredDate
      </SQL>
    </ExpressionView>
  </CalculatedColumnDef>
  <CalculatedColumnDef name='customerNumber'
    type='Numeric'>
    <ExpressionView>
      <SQL dialect='generic'>
        $customer.customerNumber
      </SQL>
    </ExpressionView>
  </CalculatedColumnDef>
  <CalculatedColumnDef name='customerCountry'
    type='String'>
    <ExpressionView>
      <SQL dialect='generic'>
        $customer.address.country
      </SQL>
    </ExpressionView>
  </CalculatedColumnDef>
  <CalculatedColumnDef name='customerName' type='String'>
    <ExpressionView>
      <SQL dialect='generic'>
        $customer.name
      </SQL>
    </ExpressionView>
  </CalculatedColumnDef>
  <CalculatedColumnDef name='productName' type='String'>
    <ExpressionView>
```

```
      <SQL dialect='generic'>
        $product.name
      </SQL>
    </ExpressionView>
  </CalculatedColumnDef>
  <CalculatedColumnDef name='productCode' type='String'>
    <ExpressionView>
      <SQL dialect='generic'>
        $product.code
      </SQL>
    </ExpressionView>
  </CalculatedColumnDef>
  <CalculatedColumnDef name='totalPrice' type='Numeric'>
    <ExpressionView>
      <SQL dialect='generic'>
        $totalPrice
      </SQL>
    </ExpressionView>
  </CalculatedColumnDef>
  <CalculatedColumnDef name='quantityOrdered'
    type='Numeric'>
    <ExpressionView>
      <SQL dialect='generic'>
        $quantityOrdered
      </SQL>
    </ExpressionView>
  </CalculatedColumnDef>
</ColumnDefs>
```

5. Save this Mondrian schema for now in your filesystem with the name
   `MongoDBPentahoCookbook.mondrian.xml`.

How it works...

In this recipe, we started creating the Mondrian 4 schema with the name
`Mondrian4MongoDBPentahoCookbook`. The first step of creating a Mondrian 4 schema is
the physical schema. The physical schema consists of a description of tables and columns in
the database. This provides the data for dimensions and cubes in the logical schema.

In a Pentaho MongoDB native connection, the physical schema is responsible for mapping
the JSON properties in the JSON documents in the collection to represent the columns of a
table. In this specific example, we created an `Orders` table with the important columns for
the OLAP schema. It's important to note that the Pentaho native connection works only for
a single collection; you can't use multiple collections to join data.

Creating a Mondrian 4 cube

This recipe shows you how to create a Mondrian 4 cube. Basically, this is the second part, after the physical model. It is responsible for mapping the business side to the physical schema.

Getting ready

Open the schema created in the previous recipe in your favorite text editor.

How to do it...

Proceed with the following steps:

1. Let's add the **Orders** cube to the schema by writing this line:

    ```
    <Cube name='Orders' defaultMeasure='Total Price'></Cube>
    ```

2. In order to add the **Product** dimension, it's necessary to write the following lines in the Cube tag:

    ```
    <Dimensions>
      <Dimension name='Product' table='Orders' key='Product
      Code'>
        <Attributes>
          <Attribute name='Name' keyColumn='productName'
            hasHierarchy='false'/>
          <Attribute name='Product Code' keyColumn=
            'productCode' hasHierarchy='false'/>
        </Attributes>
        <Hierarchies>
          <Hierarchy name='Product' hasAll='true'>
            <Level attribute='Name'/>
          </Hierarchy>
        </Hierarchies>
      </Dimension>
    </Dimensions>
    ```

3. Let's add the **Customer** dimension with the **Country** and **Name** levels by adding these lines to the **Dimensions** tag:

    ```
    <Dimension name='Customer' table='Orders' key='Product
      Code'>
      <Attributes>
    ```

```
<Attribute name='Country' keyColumn='customerCountry'
  hasHierarchy='false'/>
<Attribute name='Name' keyColumn='customerName'
  hasHierarchy='false'/>
<Attribute name='Product Code' keyColumn=
  'customerNumber' hasHierarchy='false'/>
</Attributes>
<Hierarchies>
  <Hierarchy name='Customer' hasAll='true'>
    <Level attribute='Country'/>
    <Level attribute='Name'/>
  </Hierarchy>
</Hierarchies>
</Dimension>
```

4. Now that the dimensions are declared, let's add **Measures**, **Total Price**, and **Quantity Ordered**. Insert the following lines into the **Cube** tag and after the **Dimensions** tag:

```
<MeasureGroups>
  <MeasureGroup name='Orders' table='Orders'>
    <Measures>
      <Measure name='Total Price' column='totalPrice'
        aggregator='sum' formatString='Standard'/>
      <Measure name='Quantity Ordered' column=
        'quantityOrdered' aggregator='sum'
          formatString='Standard'/>
    </Measures>
    <DimensionLinks>
      <FactLink dimension='Product'/>
      <FactLink dimension='Customer'/>
    </DimensionLinks>
  </MeasureGroup>
</MeasureGroups>
```

5. Finally, let's add the Avg Price Each calculated measure to the **Orders** cube, writing these lines inside the Cube tag and after the MeasureGroups tag:

```
<CalculatedMembers>
  <CalculatedMember name='Avg Price Each'
    dimension='Measures'>
    <Formula>IIF([Measures].[Quantity Ordered]=0,0,
      [Measures].[Total Price]/[Measures].[Quantity
        Ordered])</Formula>
```

```
      <CalculatedMemberProperty name='MEMBER_ORDINAL'
        value='9'/>
    </CalculatedMember>
  </CalculatedMembers>
```

6. Save the schema in your filesystem with the name `MongoDBPentahoCookbook.mondrian.xml`.

How it works...

In this second part, we created the proper logical cube with dimensions, measures, and calculated measures.

As we did in the previous recipes for Mondrian 3.x versions, we created two dimensions: products and customers. The product dimension has just one level, which is the name, and the customer dimension has two levels, namely the country and the customer name.

In Mondrian 4, one of the good features compared to the Mondrian 3.x version is measure groups. In Mondrian 3.x, cubes have only one `fact` physical table. If you want to create a cube with different `fact` tables joined together, you need to use a virtual cube. A virtual cube combines multiple cubes. However, this approach is no longer supported with Mondrian 4, and you need to use measure groups.

In this example, we created only one measure group. In other scenarios, it can be necessary to create more than one, with two measures: **Total Price** and **Quantity Ordered**.

After the measures, we created a calculated measure, as we did for Mondrian 3.x in previous recipes, called **Avg Price Each**. Basically, this is **Total Price** divided by **Quantity Ordered**, giving the average product price per order.

Publishing a Mondrian 4 schema

In this recipe, we will show you how to publish the Mondrian 4 schema on the Pentaho BI server, making the schema available to the Analysis Report for data exploration.

Getting ready

Make sure you have the Mondrian 4 schema that was created in the previous recipes defined well. MongoDB must be started with the databases created in the previous chapter.

How to do it...

Proceed with the following steps:

1. In your filesystem, go to `<Pentaho-installation-path>/server/biserver-ee/pentaho-solutions/system/` and open the `olap4j.properties` file with your favorite text editor.

2. Add the following lines. However, you need change the file path for the Mondrian schema; in my case, it is `/home/latino/git/pentaho-mongodb-cookbook/source code/chapter4/`. My MongoDB database has the username as `root`, and the password is `password`. If your database doesn't require authentication, you can remove it from the `connectString`. Otherwise, if your database requires authentication, you can use the `http://localhost:8080/pentaho/api/password/encrypt` endpoint to generate the encrypted password:

    ```
    cookbook.name=mongoDBPentahoCookbook
    cookbook.className=org.pentaho.platform.plugin.services.
    connections.PentahoSystemDriver cookbook.connectString=
    jdbc:mondrian4:Host=localhost;dbname=SteelWheels;
    DataServicesProvider=com.pentaho.analysis.mongo.
    MongoDataServicesProvider;Catalog=/home/latino/git/
    pentaho-mongodb-cookbook/source code/chapter4/
    MongoDBPentahoCookbook.mondrian.xml;username=root;
    password=ENC:cGFzc3dvcmQ=
    ```

3. Save the file and restart the Pentaho BI server. If you open the **Analysis Report**, you should see the new data source.

How it works...

As you notice, publishing a Mondrian 4 schema is much more manual than the Mondrian 3.x versions; you need to edit the `olap4j.properties` file. The `olap4j.properties` file consists of the Manage Data Sources of the BI server for Mondrian 4. In this file, we define the connections and the schema filesystem location. The connections are defined by a unique connection name with the following properties, with dot (`.`) splitting:

▸ `name`: This property needs to match with the Mondrian schema name:

    ```
    <Schema name='Mondrian4MongoDBPentahoCookbook'
    quoteSql='false' missingLink='ignore'
    metamodelVersion='4.00'></Schema>
    ```

▸ `className`: This is the driver class name.

- ► `connectString`: This is the olap4j connection string that contains the following properties:

  - ❏ `Host`: This is the MongoDB instance. In this example, it is the same machine, that's why we use `localhost`.

  - ❏ `dbname`: This is the MongoDB database name. In this example, it is **SteelWheels**.

  - ❏ `DataServicesProvider`: This is the MongoDB native connection data service provider.

  - ❏ `Catalog`: This is the location of the MongoDB database in the filesystem. If you have the Mondrian schema in the Pentaho repository (based on JCR), you should start the JCR path with ":", for example, `:/public`.

  - ❏ `username`: This is the username of MongoDB for the database. If the database doesn't need authentication, you can remove this property and the password property.

  - ❏ `password`: This is the MongoDB database password encrypted using the following password encryption endpoint: `http://localhost:8080/pentaho/api/password/encrypt`.

After we have the `olap4j.properties` file changed correctly, we restart the server to apply those changes. In the Pentaho BI server, you can test the Mondrian schema by selecting **Create New** and then **Analysis Report**.

5

Pentaho Reporting

In this chapter, we will cover the following:

- ▶ Copying the MongoDB JDBC library
- ▶ Connecting to MongoDB using Reporting Wizard
- ▶ Connecting to MongoDB via PDI
- ▶ Adding a chart to a report
- ▶ Adding parameters to a report
- ▶ Adding a formula to a report
- ▶ Grouping data in reports
- ▶ Creating subreports
- ▶ Creating a report with MongoDB via Java
- ▶ Publishing a report to the Pentaho server
- ▶ Running a report in the Pentaho server

Introduction

Creating printable reports for business intelligence is a keystone for any analytics solution. There are many cases where a user needs to create complex reports in various formats as well as print these reports so that they can distribute them to others throughout the business.

Pentaho Reports allows us to create connections to MongoDB in various ways to expose the crucial data stored within. We can use a number of methods to get this data from MongoDB including native connections using **Pentaho Data Integration** transformations that will get the data for us, or even Java classes that will expose the MongoDB API.

Copying the MongoDB JDBC library

We will be using some scripting in these recipes, so it's important to make sure that we have the MongoDB JDBC library copied to the correct location in the **Pentaho Report Designer**.

Getting ready

Make sure you have access to the filesystem from which you will be running the Pentaho Report Designer.

How to do it...

In this section, we will be copying a select number of libraries that will allow us to make sure that the Pentaho Report Designer can connect to MongoDB. Without these libraries we will be unable to complete the recipes in this chapter:

1. On your filesystem, navigate to `PentahoEE/design-tools/report-designer/ plugins/pentaho-mongodb-plugin/lib`.
2. Copy the `mongo-java-driver.xxx.jar` file.
3. Navigate to `PentahoEE/design-tools/report-designer/lib`.
4. Paste the `mongo-java-driver.xxx.jar` file.
5. Restart the Pentaho Report Designer.

How it works...

In this recipe, we copied the correct MongoDB libraries to the corresponding Pentaho Report Designer folder. The library that we copied was the MongoDB JDBC library that will allow us to make a connection to the MongoDB server.

Connecting to MongoDB using Reporting Wizard

In this recipe, we will guide you through the steps required to simply get data in the quickest fashion from MongoDB using a feature of the Pentaho Report Designer called the **Report Designer Wizard**. This wizard helps us to define our connection to the MongoDB data source, as well as to define a query that is to be executed to get data into our report.

Getting ready

To get ready for this recipe, you first need to start the MongoDB server with the same database as in the last chapter. You will also want to start the Pentaho Report Designer.

The Pentaho **Report Designer** is started in Windows as follows:

This can be done via the Windows Start menu by navigating to **Start** | **All Programs** | **Pentaho Enterprise Edition** | **Design Tools** | **Report Designer** and then by clicking on the report designer icon.

The Pentaho **Report Designer** is started in Linux as follows:

Open up a terminal and navigate to the `PentahoEE/design-tools/report-designer` folder. Execute the `report-designer` bash script using `./report-designer.sh`.

When the **Report Designer** loads, you should be presented with a **Welcome** screen.

How to do it...

In this section, we are going to create a simple report using the Pentaho Report Design Wizard and the data from MongoDB:

1. Click on the **Report Wizard** button on the Pentaho Report splash screen:

2. Select **Cobalt Template** and click on **Next**:

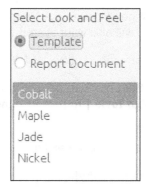

3. Add a new data source by clicking on the plus icon in the top-right corner of the window:

4. Select **MongoDB** from the pop-up list of data sources.

5. Add a new query by clicking on the plus icon in the top-left corner of the window.

6. Give the **Query** a name like **Orders**.

7. Set the **Host** property to **localhost**.

8. Set the **Port** property to **27017**.

9. By default, you do not need to specify a username or password for a default MongoDB installation:

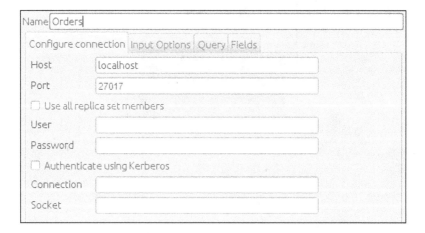

10. Select the **Input Options** tab.

11. Click on the **Get DBs** button to return a list of available **Databases** in the MongoDB connections.

12. Select the **SteelWheels** Databases.

13. Click on the **Get Collections** button to return a list of available MongoDB collections in the databases.

14. Select the **Orders** collections from the list:

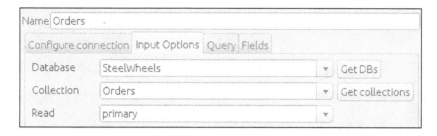

15. Click on the **Query** tab.

16. Copy and paste the following query into the **Query Expression (JSON)** text area:

```
{
  $query: {},
  $orderby: {
    customer.address.country:1,
    customer.address.city:1,
    product.line:1,
  }
}
```

17. Copy and paste the following filter into the **Fields Expression (JSON)** input:

```
{
  customer.address.country:1,
  customer.address.city:1,
  product.line:1,
```

```
    totalPrice:1
}
```

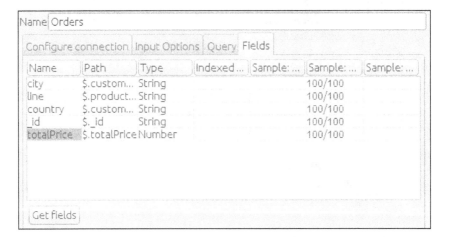

Name Orders

Configure connection | Input Options | Query | Fields

Query expression (JSON)

```
{
            $query: {},
            $orderby: {
                        customer.address.country:1,
                        customer.address.city:1,
                        product.line:1,

            }
}
```

☐ Query is aggregation pipeline

Fields expression (JSON) 1, customer.address.city:1, product.line:1, totalPrice:1 }

18. Click on the **Fields** tab.

19. Click on the **Get fields** button, as shown in the following screenshot:

Name Orders

Configure connection | Input Options | Query | Fields

Name	Path	Type	Indexed...	Sample: ...	Sample: ...	Sample: ...
city	$.custom...	String			100/100	
line	$.product...	String			100/100	
country	$.custom...	String			100/100	
_id	$._id	String			100/100	
totalPrice	$.totalPrice	Number			100/100	

Get fields

20. Click on **Preview**. You should see five fields of data ordered by country, city, and then product line:

21. Click on **OK** to exit the **Query Wizard**.

Now that the query has been defined, you should return to the main **Report Wizard** window with your query available to be selected.

1. Select your query from the **Data Source** list:

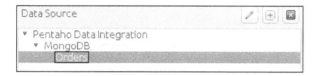

2. Click on **Next**.

3. Select **country**, **city**, **line**, and **totalPrice** from the available fields and add these fields to the selected fields' area by clicking on the arrow next to the **Selected** box. These are the fields we want to add to the report.

4. Change the **order** of these fields so that they are listed from top to bottom as **country**, **city**, **line**, and **totalPrice**:

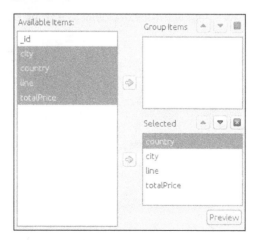

5. Click on **Finish** to exit the **Report Wizard**.

How it works...

The **Report Wizard** allows us to simply create a query and configure it to return the correct data in a couple of steps. Once we have the data from the query, we can then select what fields will be included in the report. With the query and report defined in the **Report Wizard**, we will be able to generate a report in the Pentaho **Report Designer** that will get us quickly started. From this point, we are free to edit the generated report further using the various tools that come with the Pentaho Report Designer.

Connecting to MongoDB via PDI

In this recipe, we will guide you through the steps required to connect to a MongoDB instance using a Pentaho Data Integration transformation and execute that transformation in a Pentaho Report.

Getting ready

To get ready for this recipe, you will have to make sure your MongoDB instance is running.

How to do it...

For this recipe, we are going to use a transformation that we have already developed for the book that will return a list of orders as shown in the previous recipe. We are also going to build this report manually instead of using the Report Wizard:

1. In **Report Designer**, go to **File | New.**
2. Click on the **Data** tab in the top-right corner of **Report Designer**.
3. Right-click on the **Data** item in the list and select **Pentaho Data Integration**:

4. Just like previously in the **Report Wizard**, we are going to create our data source:

    1. To add a new data source, click on the **Plus Icon** in the top-left corner of the pop-up window.

    2. Set the **Name** property of the query to **Orders.**

    3. Click on the **Browse** button to open the select transformation dialog.

    4. Browse to the `chapter 5` folder and select the `chapter5-getorders.ktr` transformation. (This file is provided as source code along with this book.)

    5. Select the **OUT** step in the list of steps available in this transformation:

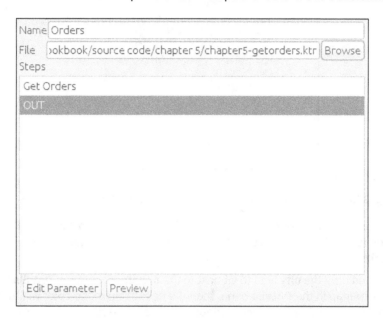

6. Click on **Preview**, as shown in the preceding screenshot. The **Preview** window shows up as seen in the following screenshot:

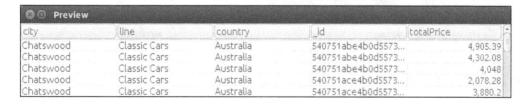

7. Click on **OK**.

We have now chosen our data source. We can see the fields that are available to us in the **Data** tab of Report Designer:

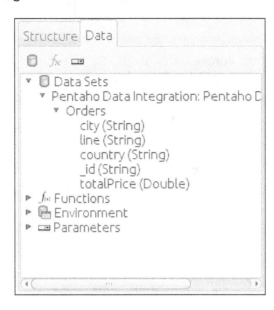

The next step is to get these fields into the report. To do this, we will follow these simple steps:

1. Click and drag the **country** field from the **Data** tab and drop it into the **Details** band of the report, just to make sure that the item is aligned to the top-left side of the **Details** band.

2. Click and drag the **city** field to sit next to the **country** field in the **Details** band. If the items overlap in the **Details** band, then the item background color will turn pink. This is to inform you that you have overlapping items in the report.

3. Finally, click and drag the remaining **line** and **totalPrice** fields into the report and set them alongside the previous fields. Once the items are in the correct position, you should be looking at something that will be similar to the following screenshot:

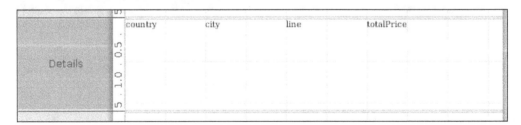

4. Click on **Preview** and the following report appears:

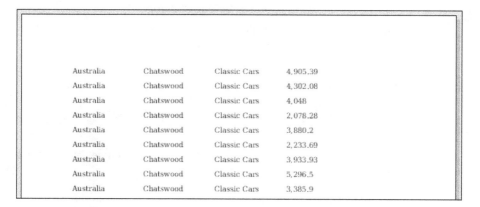

Australia	Chatswood	Classic Cars	4,905.39
Australia	Chatswood	Classic Cars	4,302.08
Australia	Chatswood	Classic Cars	4,048
Australia	Chatswood	Classic Cars	2,078.28
Australia	Chatswood	Classic Cars	3,880.2
Australia	Chatswood	Classic Cars	2,233.69
Australia	Chatswood	Classic Cars	3,933.93
Australia	Chatswood	Classic Cars	5,296.5
Australia	Chatswood	Classic Cars	3,385.9

How it works...

This report simply executes a Pentaho Data Integration that connects to a MongoDB data source to return data. Once the data is in the report, we can define what fields we want to display from the transformation in our report.

Adding a chart to a report

In this recipe, we will guide you through the steps required to fetch data from a MongoDB instance and render a Pentaho chart into the report. Similar to the previous recipe, we will be using a Pentaho Data Integration transformation to get order summary data to populate the chart. This data will consist of total order values grouped by country.

Getting ready

To get ready for this recipe, you will have to make sure your MongoDB instance is running.

How to do it...

1. In **Report Designer**, go to **File | New**.
2. Click on the **Data** tab in the top-right corner of **Report Designer**.
3. Right-click on the **Data** item in the list and select **Pentaho Data Integration**.
4. To add a new data source, click on the plus button in the top-left corner of the pop-up window.

5. Set the **Name** property of the query to **Orders**.

6. Click on the **Browse** button to open the **Select transformation** dialog.

7. Browse your file system and select the `chapter5-getorders-summary.ktr` transformation, as done in the previous recipe. (This file is provided as source code along with this book.)

8. Select the **OUT** step in the list of steps available in this transformation.

9. Click on **Preview**.

10. Click on **OK**.

You will notice that the **Orders** data is broken down into countries this time. We have used a simple **Group By** step in the transformation to do this.

Now that we have our data, we can use it to populate a simple bar chart in the Pentaho Report:

1. Drag a chart component from the Pentaho Report Designer toolbar to the left of the **Report Header** band:

2. Align the chart component to fit the width of the report. You will have to resize the anchors to do this:

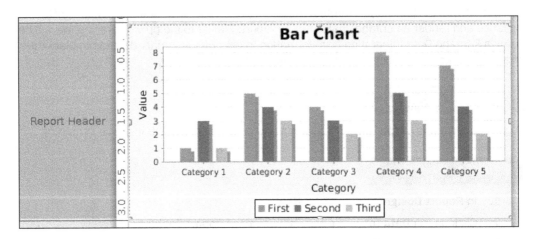

3. Double-click on the chart component that you placed into the **Report Header** band. This will open **Chart Properties**.

4. Make sure you are looking at the **Primary Data Source** tab.

    1. Set **category-column** to **country**.

    2. Set **value-columns** to **totalPrice.**

    3. Set **auto-generated-series** to **true**.

The following screenshot appears:

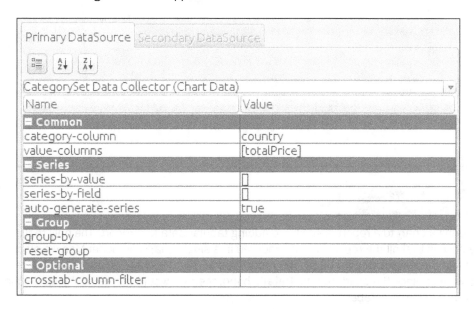

5. Click on **OK.**

6. Click on **Previe**w to see the report.

If everything goes well, you will be looking at a simple chart in the **Report Header** band. Before we finish up, we can set a couple of common options to make the chart look a little more pleasing to the eye:

1. Double-click on the **Chart Component**

2. You should see a large list of various options on the left-hand side panel.

3. Set **Chart Title** to **Orders by Country**.

4. Set **X Axis Label Rotation** to **90**.

    The following screenshot shows the final output chart:

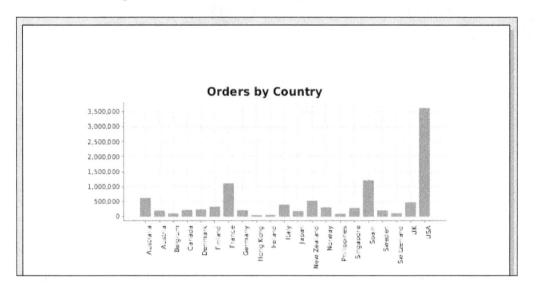

How it works...

Rendering a chart to a report is similar to adding tabular data to a report. The only real difference is that all the report data is rendered in a single chart component, so we place our chart into the **Report Header** band. The report header band is only executed once per report. If we were to place the chart into the **Details** band, then we would be seeing the same chart for every row in the database.

Reporting charts have many options. Feel free to open the chart component and play around with the other options available to you.

Adding parameters to a report

In this recipe, we will guide you through the steps required to pass parameters to a report based on a MongoDB query. Using parameters in our reports means that we can filter data from the data source so that users can find the information that they need faster than a report with ALL data. To do this, we are going to add a parameter to the report first and then parameterize our MongoDB query.

Getting ready

To get ready for this recipe, you will have to make sure your MongoDB instance is running.

How to do it...

Let's start by adding a parameter to the report:

1. In Report Designer, go to **File | New**.
2. Click on the **Data** tab in the top-right corner of **Report Designer**.
3. Right-click on the **Parameters** item in the list and select **Add Parameter...**:

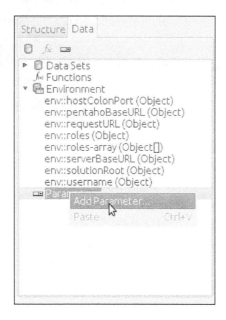

We are going to need a small data source that will populate our parameter dropdown with values that the user can send to the MongoDB query. We can generate a data source using a table. Let's do that now:

1. To add a new data source, click on the plus button in the top-left corner of the pop-up window.
2. Select **Table** from the list of available data source types.

3. Click on the plus button in the top-right corner of the pop-up window to add a new blank table query.

4. Set **Query Name** to **Countries.**

5. In the **Table,** click on the **ID** header cell and then click on the **Remove column** button at the top-right side of the table. This will remove the **ID** field from the table and leave only the **Value** field. In this case, this is all we want: a table that contains a single list of countries.

6. Click on the cell below the **Value** header of the table and set the first row to **USA**.

7. Click on the **Add Empty Row** button at the top of the table to add a new row to the **Table** data source.

8. Click on the cell below the **USA** row and set **Value** to **UK**.

9. Once completed, your table query should look like the following screenshot:

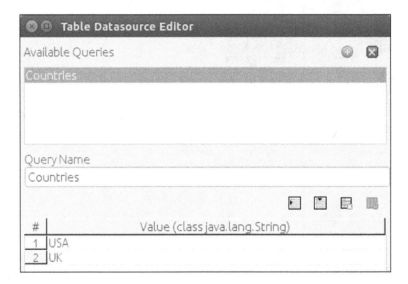

10. Click on **OK** to return to the **Parameter Configuration** popup.

Now that we have a simple table-based data source, we can configure the parameter to use this data source to populate a filter component:

1. Set the **Name** property to **PARAM_COUNTRY**.

2. Set the **Label** property to **Select Country**.

3. Set the **Default Value** property to **USA**.

4. In the prompt section, set **Display Type** to **Drop Down**.

5. Set **Query** to **Countries**.

6. Your parameter configuration should look like the following screenshot:

7. Click on **OK**.

At this point, we are free to preview the report. There will be no data in the report, but you should be able to test the filter we just added. At the moment, when you are making a selection, it is internally setting the value of **PARAM_COUNTRY** to whatever you choose. The next step is to send this **PARAM_COUNTRY** value to a MongoDB query:

1. Click on the **Data** tab in the top-right corner of **Report Designer**.

2. Right-click on the data item in the list and select **MongoDB.**

3. To add a new data source, click on the **Plus** button in the top-left corner of the pop-up window.

4. Give the **Query** a name like **Orders.**

5. Set the **Host** property to **localhost.**

6. Set the **Port** property to **27017.**

7. You do not need to specify a username or password.

8. Select the **Input Options** tab.

9. Click on the **Get DBs** button to return a list of available databases in the MongoDB connections.

10. Select the **SteelWheels** database.

11. Click on the **Get Collections** button to return a list of available MongoDB collections in the databases.

12. Select the **Orders** collections from the list.

13. Click on the **Query** tab.

14. Copy and paste the following query into the **Query Expression (JSON)** text area:

```
{
  $query: {},
  $orderby: {
    customer.address.country:1,
    customer.address.city:1,
    product.line:1,
  }
}
```

15. Copy and paste the following filter into the **Fields Expression (JSON)** input:

```
{
  customer.address.country:1,
  customer.address.city:1,
  product.line:1,
  totalPrice:1
}
```

16. Click on the **Fields** tab.

17. Click on the **Get Fields** button.

18. Click on **Preview.**

You would see data from a static query similar to the one we used for **Report Design Wizard**. The next step is to parameterize this query to accept the **PARAM_COUNTRY** value from the report filter:

1. Click on the query table and edit the query to so that it looks like the following snippet. Note the text in bold:

```
{
  $query: {customer.address.country:"${PARAM_COUNTRY}"},
  $orderby: {
    customer.address.country:1,
```

```
        customer.address.city:1,
        product.line:1,
    }
}
```

2. Click on **OK**.

You will notice that we have made a small change to the query. In this case, we are going to place the value of **PARAM_COUNTY** in the query. There is one last step to complete this:

1. Right-click on the **Orders MongoDB** query in the **Data** tab and click on **Edit Query**.

2. Click on the **Edit Parameters** section at the bottom of the popup.

You should see **PARAM_COUNTRY** listed in the **Parameters** table. This is the value in the MongoDB query. We need to specify what to replace this value with. In our case, it is the value that comes from our filter:

1. Click on the cell in **Value** column.

2. Set it to **=[PARAM_COUNTRY]**.

3. Click on **OK** to close the **Parameters** popup:

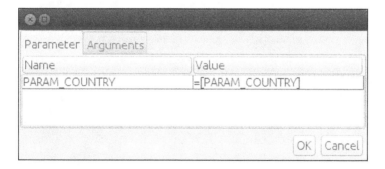

4. Click on **OK** to close the MongoDB data source popup.

We're nearly there. Our parameter/filter is working in the report, and our MongoDB query has been linked to the parameter. One final thing to do is to actually add some fields from the MongoDB data source to the actual report layout:

1. Click and drag the **country** field from the **Data** tab and drop it into the **Details** band of the report, just to make sure that the item is aligned to the top-left side of the **Details** band.

2. Click and drag the **city** field to sit next to the **country** field in the **Details** band. If the items overlap in the **Details** band, then the item background color will turn pink. This is to inform you that you have overlapping items in the report.

3. Finally, click and drag the remaining **line** and **totalPrice** fields into the report and set them alongside the previous fields. Once the items are in the correct position, you should be looking at something that is similar to the following screenshot:

4. Click on **Preview**. The following screenshot then appears:

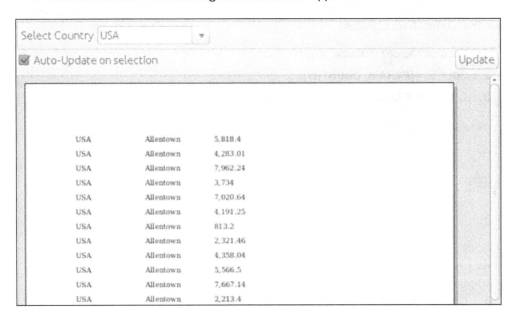

The report should render data from the MongoDB data source for The USA only. This is the default value of our parameter filter. You can change the filter option and the report will refresh to display only the UK data.

How it works...

We add a parameter to the report that is populated by a table-based data source. This selector will set the value of PARAM_COUNTRY to whatever the user selects. The value is then passed down to the MongoDB query that has been written to accept the parameter. When the user makes a selection from the filter, the report is rerun and the correct data is fetched from the MongoDB data source.

Adding a formula to a report

In this recipe, we will guide you through the steps required to add a simple formula to your reports. Adding a formula to a report can help you do things that might not be possible to do directly in your query. They can also help with other cool features such as conditional formatting. A formula in Pentaho Report Designer is similar to a formula in an Excel document. If you understand Excel, then this section will be easy for you!

Getting ready

To get ready for this recipe, you will have to make sure your MongoDB instance is running.

How to do it...

We will start off by loading a report that was created in an earlier recipe. Don't worry if you never completed the recipe, as we have a copy of it. Perform the following steps:

1. Go to **File** | **Open**.

2. Navigate the file system to find the `chatpter5-orders-report.prpt` file. (This file is provided as source code along with this book.)

3. Click on **Preview** to get the following screenshot:

Australia	Chatswood	Classic Cars	4,905.39
Australia	Chatswood	Classic Cars	4,302.08
Australia	Chatswood	Classic Cars	4,048
Australia	Chatswood	Classic Cars	2,078.28
Australia	Chatswood	Classic Cars	3,880.2
Australia	Chatswood	Classic Cars	2,233.69
Australia	Chatswood	Classic Cars	3,933.93
Australia	Chatswood	Classic Cars	5,296.5
Australia	Chatswood	Classic Cars	3,385.9

You should be looking at a simple report that lists orders placed for certain products and countries. We are going to add a formula that will set the background color of a sales value if it is above a certain value. This sort of formula can be useful for many reports! This will be done as follows:

1. Click on the **totalPrice** field in the **Details** band of the report.
2. Click on the **Structure** tab in the top-right of Report Designer.

Below the **Structure/Data** panel, you will see another panel with **Style** and **Attributes** tabs. Since we want to dynamically set the color of the field, we will add a formula to the **Style** attribute:

1. Click on the **Style** tab.
2. Scroll down the list until you see **bg-color**. It will be nested within the **text style** category.
3. Click on the green plus icon next to the **bg-color** field. This will open the formula editor:

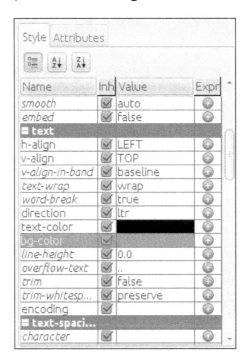

4. In the **Formula** property, you can copy and paste the following text:

   =IF([totalPrice]>5000;"Red";"Green")

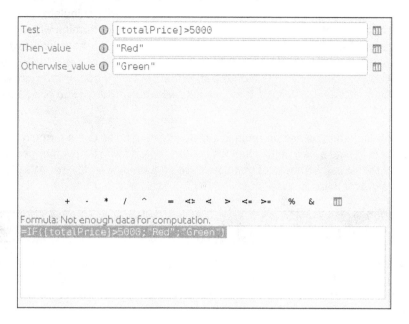

5. Click on **OK**.

6. Preview the report to get the following screenshot:

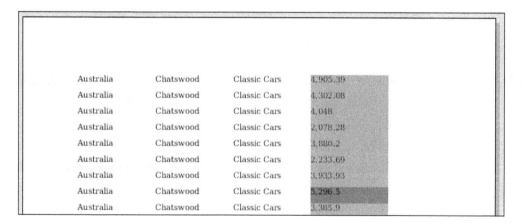

How it works...

In this simple recipe, we have created a formula that allows us to manipulate the background color of a data field. We are using an `IF` function to determine whether the value of the field is over a certain value, and depending on this, we return the color we want that field to be in. We are executing this formula in the `bg-color` style of the field. We could also, for example, use the same `IF` function on the style that controls whether the field should be in bold. Instead of returning a color in that example, we would return `true` or `false` (should the field be bold or not).

We are not only limited to using a formula in a style. We could also use a formula to do other things such as calculate a new field value. We could simply add an empty number field to a report and set the `Value` attribute of that field to be something like `= [FieldA] + [FieldB]`. This can be useful for inline calculations.

Grouping data in reports

In this recipe, we will take you through the steps required to display raw data into groups. This can be useful if we want to create *group sum* functions. In this recipe, we will order the data into groups of counties and cities. This will then allow us to add sums for each city or country group.

Getting ready

To get ready for this recipe, you will have to make sure your MongoDB instance is running.

How to do it...

We are going to use a PDI transformation to populate the report from a previous recipe. This transformation will give us a list of orders by country, city, and product line:

1. In **Report Designer**, navigate to **File | New.**
2. Click on the **Data** tab in the top-right corner of Report Designer.
3. Right-click on the **Data** item in the list and select **Pentaho Data Integration.**
4. To add a new data source, click the plus button in the top-left corner of the pop-up window.
5. Set the **Name** property of the query to **Orders.**
6. Click on the **Browse** button to open the **Select transformation** dialog.
7. Select the **chapter5-getorders.ktr** transformation.

8. Select the **OUT** step in the list of steps available in this transformation.

9. Click on **Preview.**

10. Click on **OK.**

Now that we have defined the query we want, you might think the next step would be to drag the data fields into the report. Before we do this, we are going to define our report groups. These report groups add new report bands to the report in which we can place our data:

1. Click on the **Structure** tab in the top-right corner of Report Designer.

2. Select **Edit Groups**. This will open up the **Group Configuration** popup.

3. You will see two fields in a table. One is called **Name** and the other is called **Fields**.

4. Double-click on the first item in the **Name** column called **::group-0.**

5. Set this value to **GROUP_COUNTRY.**

6. In the **Fields** section click on the **...** button to browse the available fields in the report.

7. A new popup will appear. Scroll through the list of **Available Fields** and select **country.**

8. Click on the **Right Arrow** button to move the **country** field to the **Selected Fields** area.

9. Click on **OK**. The following screenshot shows the **Edit Group** window:

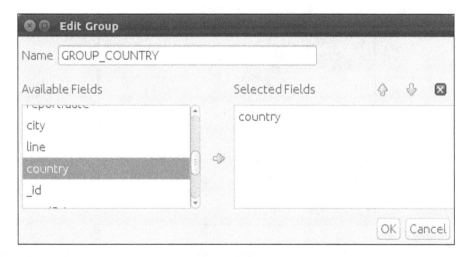

10. We have now configured our first group. It should look like the following screenshot:

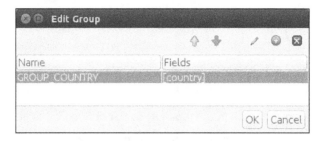

11. Click on **OK** to exit the **Edit Groups** popup.

We may have added the group to the report; however, no new bands are visible on the report canvas. The group exists, but by default, it is hidden from view. The next step we need to do is show this group band on the report:

1. In the **Structure** tab, navigate and select the **Group Header** band:

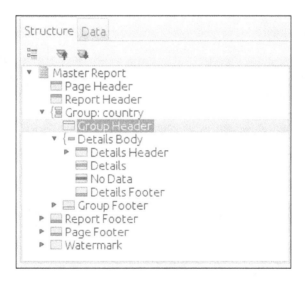

2. In the **Attributes** tab beside the **Structure** tab, we are looking for a property called **hide-on-canvas**.

3. Change the value of **hide-on-canvas** to **false** as shown in the following screenshot:

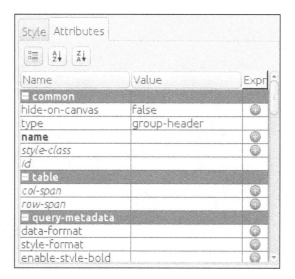

You will notice that a new report band will appear on the canvas called **Group Header.**

We are now ready to start adding our data to this report. We are going to add the **country** field to the **Report Header** band and the rest of the data fields to the **Details** band:

1. Click on the **Data** tab in the top-right of Report Designer.

2. Drag the **country** field into the **Group Header** band on the report canvas.

3. Set the **font size** for this field a little bigger than the default and also set it to **bold.**

4. Drag the **city, line,** and **totalPrice** fields to the **Details** band of the report canvas:

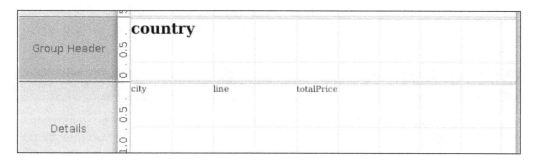

5. Click on Preview.

You should have a report that now has data grouped by country as shown in the following screenshot:

Australia

Chatswood	Classic Cars	4,905.39
Chatswood	Classic Cars	4,302.08
Chatswood	Classic Cars	4,048
Chatswood	Classic Cars	2,078.28
Chatswood	Classic Cars	3,880.2
Chatswood	Classic Cars	2,233.69

How it works...

In this recipe, we are simply getting ordered data from a PDI transformation and grouping it using the Pentaho Report Designer. The **Details** band loops for every record that is returned by the data source. The **Group** band hover has been configured only to look for each country. Using this, we are able to drop the **country** field into the **Group Header** band and we can see that it is only displayed once for each country in the data source.

It's also possible to created nested groups in the report. We could have added another group to this report and looped over the **city** field.

Before we finish, it's also worth mentioning that without groups, we can also place items in the **Group Footer** band. Similar to **Group Header**, this band is disabled by default, but we can enable it in the **Group Footer Attributes** section. Once enabled, we could place sum functions to give us the totals for each group or subgroup that allow us to create much more complex reports.

Creating subreports

A subreport is a report that is embedded within the master report. There are many reasons for which we might do this. One of the reasons would be to add a chart to a master report that runs a different data source. It's worth mentioning that we can only run a single data source per report. If we wanted to create a report that not only lists the orders in detail but also displays a chart for the summary of the orders, then we would have to create a subreport. The subreport would contain the chart for the summary, and we would include this subreport in the master report.

Getting ready

To get ready for this recipe, you will have to make sure your MongoDB instance is running.

How to do it...

We are going to use two PDI transformations to populate the report from the previous recipes. These transformations will give us a list of orders by country, city, and product line, as well as a summary of orders grouped by country that we will use for our chart in the subreport:

1. In **Report Designer**, go to **File | New**.
2. Click on the **Data** tab in the top-right corner of Report Designer.
3. Right-click on the **Data** item in the list and select **Pentaho Data Integration**.
4. To add a new data source, click on the plus button in the top-left corner of the pop-up window.
5. Set the **Name** property of the query to **Orders.**
6. Click on the **Browse** button to open the **Select Transformation** dialog.
7. Select the **chapter5-getorders** transformation.
8. Select the **OUT** step in the list of steps available in this transformation.
9. Click on **Preview.**
10. Click on **OK.**

We have mentioned before that we are also going to need the summary orders data source to populate the chart in our subreport. We are going to add the summary orders data source to the master report and then pass it down to the subreport to populate the chart. Let's add the secondary data source to the master report right now:

1. Click on the **Data** tab in the top-right corner of Report Designer.
2. Right-click on the **Data** item in the list and select **Pentaho Data Integration**.
3. To add a new data source, click the **Plus** button in the top-left corner of the pop-up window.
4. Set the **Name** property of the query to **OrdersSummary**.
5. Click on the **Browse** button to open the **Select Transformation** dialog.
6. Select the **chapter5-getorders-summary** transformation.
7. Select the **OUT** step in the list of steps available in this transformation.
8. Click on **Preview.**
9. Click on **OK.**

We should now be looking at a report with two data sources available. The **Orders** data source has been selected by default for the master report because we added it first. The **Orders Summary** data source is just sitting idle at the moment. We can tell which data source is selected for a report if we can see the fields listed in that data source, as shown in the following screenshot:

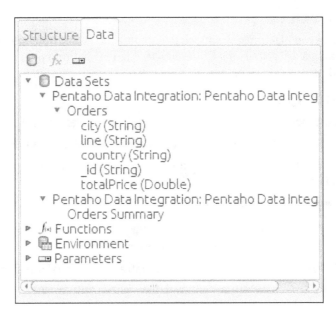

Let's populate the master report with data from the **Orders** query:

1. Click and drag the **country** field from the **Data** tab and drop it into the **Details** band of the report just to make sure that the item is aligned to the top-left side of the **Details** band.

2. Click and drag the **city** field to sit next to the **country** field in the **Details** band. If the items overlap in the **Details** band, then the item background color will turn pink. This is to inform you that you have overlapping items in the report.

3. Finally, click and drag the remaining **line** and **totalPrice** fields into the report and set them alongside the previous fields.

At this point, we can preview our report and it will display data for the **Orders** data source. Let's move on to the subreport.

The subreport, as we have mentioned before, will contain a single chart that is populated from the **Order Summary** data source in the master report. We want this **Orders Summary** chart to only appear once at the top of our final report. This will give the user a breakdown of the **Orders** data contained in the rest of the report:

1. Drag **Sub Report Component** from the toolbar on the left into the report canvas and drop it into the **Report Header** band.

2. A popup will appear asking whether you want an **inline** or **banded** subreport. Click on **banded**. This will set the subreport to take the full width of the parent band.

3. Another popup will appear asking you which data source you want to pass from the master report to the subreport. Click the **Orders Summary** data source.

4. Click on **OK**.

After you click on **OK**, you should be looking at a new report tab next to the master report. This subreport acts like any other regular report with the only difference being that it is technically contained within the master report.

Let's add a chart to this subreport:

1. Drag a chart component from the toolbar on the left into the **Report Header** band of the subreport.

2. Resize the **Chart Component** so that it has a decent width and height.

3. Double-click on the **Chart Component** in Report Header.

4. In the **Primary Data Source** tab, set the **Category** column property to **country**.

5. Set the **Value** column property to **totalPrice**.

6. Set the **auto-generated-series** property to **true**.

7. Click on **OK**.

Now that we have defined our chart and set the correct field for the data source, we can click on the **Preview Report** button. If you preview in the subreport, it will actually preview the master report.

You should be seeing something like the following screenshot:

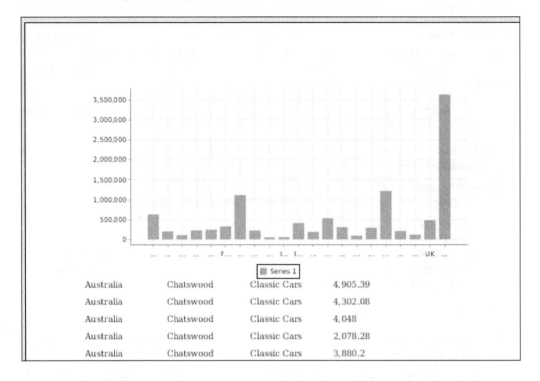

How it works...

Subreports are nested within the master report. We define ALL data sources in the master report and specify which data sources we want to use when we add subreports to the master report.

The subreport has all the functionality of the master report. We could even go as far as to specify a more complex subreport that contains a lower granularity of data. This subreport would generate many rows and would then be embedded into the master report.

There is no limit to how many subreports you can add to a master report, although things can start to get complex pretty quickly if you are not careful.

Creating a report with MongoDB via Java

There are times when we might need more control over our MongoDB data source. In cases like these, it's possible to execute a MongoDB query using BeanShell. This allows us to call up the MongoDB JDBC classes to execute the query manually.

Getting ready

To get ready for this recipe, you will have to make sure your MongoDB instance is running.

How to do it...

We are going to add a new advanced data source:

1. In **Report Designer**, navigate to **File | New**.
2. Click on the **Data** tab in the top-right corner of Report Designer.
3. Right-click on the **Datasets** item in the list, select **Advanced**, and then **Scriptable**.
4. Select the **beanshell** language from the panel on the left-hand side.
5. Add a new value using the green plus icon.
6. Set the **Name** query to **Orders.**
7. Copy and paste the following script into the **Query** window:

```
import com.mongodb.*;
import org.pentaho.reporting.engine.classic.core.util.
TypedTableModel;
Mongo mongo = new Mongo("localhost", 27017);
db = mongo.getDB("SteelWheels");
orders = db.getCollection("Orders");
String[] columnNames = {"Country", "City", "Line", "TotalPrice"};
Class[] columnTypes = {String.class, String.class, String.class,
Double.class};
TypedTableModel model = new TypedTableModel(columnNames,
columnTypes);

BasicDBObject dbo = new BasicDBObject();

docs= orders.find(dbo);

while (docs.hasNext()) {
  doc = docs.next();
  model.addRow(new Object[] {
    doc.get("customer").get("address").get("country"),
    doc.get("customer").get("address").get("city"),
    doc.get("product").get("line"),
    doc.get("totalPrice")
  });
}
```

```
docs.close();
return model;
```

8. Click on **Preview**.

9. Click on **OK**.

You can see from the preview window that we are able to return the data directly from MongoDB with a combination of the MongoDB Java classes and some BeanShell scripting. We can now drag the fields from the data source into the **Report Designer** canvas.

1. Click and drag the **country** field from the **Data** tab and drop it into the **Details** band of the report just to make sure that the item is aligned to the top-left corner of the **Details** band.

2. Click and drag the **city** field so that it is next to the **country** field in the **Details** band. If the items overlap in the **Details** band, then the item background color will turn pink. This is to inform you that you have overlapping items in the report.

3. Finally, click and drag the remaining **line** and **totalPrice** fields into the report and set them alongside the previous fields.

How it works...

In this recipe, we simply added a new scriptable data source to our report. We imported the required MongoDB and Reporting libraries that include the MongoDB JDBC classes and wrote a query that would connect to our MongoDB instance, return a result set, and then merge this result set into an object that the Pentaho Report Designer can understand. When the query is executed, we get back a list of fields that come from this object.

Publishing a report to the Pentaho server

Running reports in the **Preview** mode via Report Designer is all well and good; however, for the solution to really be useful, we should publish it to the Pentaho server so that other users can run our reports via a web browser.

Getting ready

To get ready for this recipe, you will have to make sure your MongoDB instance is running.

How to do it...

We are going to open a report from a previous chapter and publish it to the Pentaho server:

1. Go to **File | Open**.
2. Select the **chaptet5-orders-report.prpt** directory.
3. Click on **Preview**.

You should be able to simply run this report and see the **Orders** data. Now it's time to publish the report:

1. Go to **File | Publish** or press *Ctrl + Shift + P*.
2. You will need to authenticate with the Pentaho server. Make sure that the following properties are set:
   1. **URL** is set to `http://localhost:8080/pentaho`.
   2. **User** is set to `admin`.
   3. **Password** is set to `password`.
3. Click on **OK**.

The following screenshot shows the **Login** page:

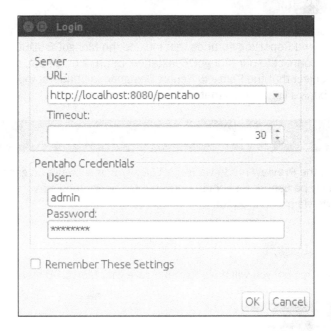

4. In the next pop-up window, we will choose the location where we want to save our report and also choose the options that should be set as default:

   1. Navigate to the **Public | SteelWheels** directory.

   2. Set the **Title** property to **Orders Report**.

   3. Set **Output Type** to **HTML (Stream)**.

5. Click on **OK**.

The report will now be published to the Pentaho server. If all goes well, you will get a confirmation message asking whether you want to run the report now. Click on **No**:

How it works...

To publish a report to the Pentaho server, we have to first authenticate with the Pentaho server. If the details are correct, we can choose a location and some options for how the report should run by default. In this case, we set the default **Output Type** to be **HTML**. The user still has the ability to choose other **Output Types** during the execution of the report on the server.

Running a report in the Pentaho server

In this recipe, you will learn how to run an **Orders** report on the Pentaho server.

Getting ready

Make sure that you have started your Pentaho BA Server using the server control scripts. You should be able to access the server via your favorite web browser with the following URL: `http://localhost:8080/`

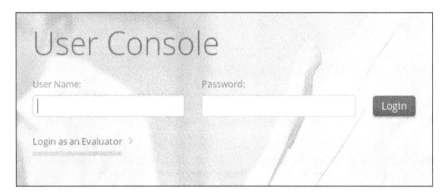

How to do it...

We are going to log in to the BI Server to run the report.

1. Navigate to the Pentaho server login screen using your favorite web browser. Use the following login details:

   ❑ Username: `admin`

   ❑ Password: `password`

2. Click on **Browse Files** on the main screen.

3. In the **Folder** hierarchy tree, expand **Public**, and then click on the **Steel Wheels** folder.

4. In the **Files** section, you will see a list of reports including **Orders Report**.

5. Double-click on **Orders Report** to open it as shown in the following screenshot:

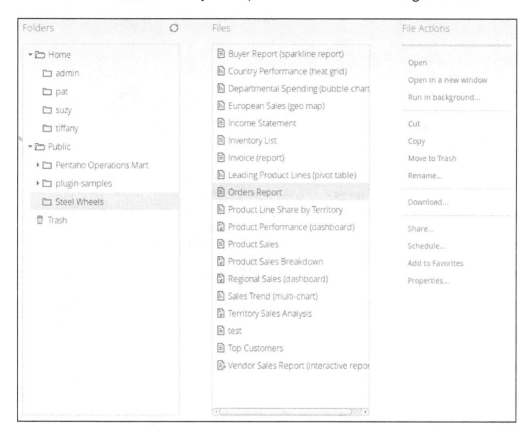

6. Once you double-click on the report, it will open and execute in the **HTML** format by default. You can run the report in PDF if you like:

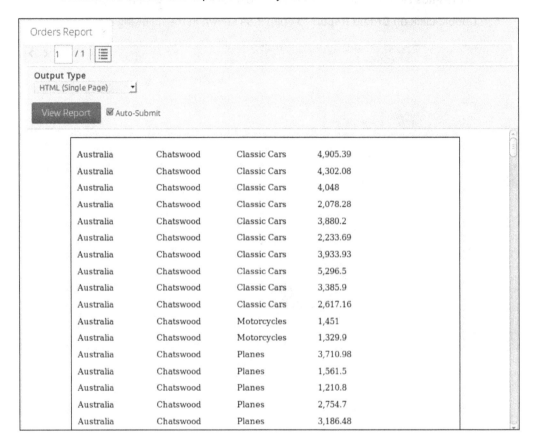

7. Set the **Output Type** to **PDF**.

The report will execute once you have made the selection. This is the default operation of the reports. You can uncheck the **Auto Submit** option if you have more parameters in your report that you would like to set *before* the report is executed. After this, you can click on the **View Report** button.

How it works...

Once reports are published to the Pentaho server, it's a simple case of double-clicking on the reports to execute them. You can then choose the values for the report parameters before you execute the report a second time.

6

The Pentaho BI Server

In this chapter, we will cover the following recipes:

- ▸ Importing Foodmart MongoDB sample data
- ▸ Creating a new analysis view using Pentaho Analyzer
- ▸ Creating a dashboard using Pentaho Dashboard Designer

Introduction

The Pentaho Community Edition, by default, comes with plugins for developing solutions (dashboards, reports, and so on) without end user plugins. However, it's possible to find some plugins for the target audience in the Pentaho marketplace.

Pentaho EE offers some end user plugins such as Pentaho Analyzer and Pentaho Dashboard Designer. With these two plugins, users are able to easily create visualizations from different data sources using a web interface. In this chapter, you will learn how to explore and create visualizations of your MongoDB data using Pentaho Analyzer, and how to create dashboards using Pentaho Dashboard Designer.

Importing Foodmart MongoDB sample data

In this recipe, you will learn how to import one of the most famous databases in the Pentaho community, the Foodmart database, into MongoDB. The Foodmart database has been used to demonstrate the diverse features available in Pentaho. The sample data for MongoDB is available in the Pentaho EE version, and it is possible use the Pentaho MongoDB native connection to perform an analysis on top of the database.

Getting ready

To get ready for this recipe, you will need Pentaho EE installed, and make sure that you have the MongoDB server running with the data from the previous chapters.

How to do it...

Let's import the sample using the command line. Perform the following steps:

1. Importing the MongoDB Foodmart database into a Windows environment:

    1. Uncompress the ZIP file at `<pentaho-installation>/server/biserver-ee/pentaho-solutions/system/samples/mondrian-data-foodmart-json-<version>.zip` in the same location.

    2. Create a `.bat` file named `import.bat` inside the folder with the JSON source files. Insert the following content into the file and replace `<mongodb-path>` with the location of your MongoDB server:

    ```
    @echo off
    for %%f in (*.json) do (
    if "%%f" == "sales_fact_1997_collapsed.json" (
    echo "--db foodmart --collection sales --file %%~nf.json"
    "<mongodb-path>\bin\mongoimport.exe" --db foodmart
    --collection sales --file %%~nf.json
    )
    echo "--db foodmart --collection %%~nf --file %%~nf.json"
    "<mongodb-path>\bin\mongoimport.exe" --db foodmart
    --collection %%~nf --file %%~nf.json
    )
    ```

    3. After some minutes, you will be able to check out the Foodmart data using Mongo shell.

2. Importing MongoDB Foodmart database in a Linux environment:

    1. Uncompress the ZIP file at `<pentaho-installation>/server/biserver-ee/pentaho-solutions/system/samples/mondrian-data-foodmart-json-<version>.zip` in the same location.

    2. Create a bash script file named `import.sh` inside of the folder that contains the JSON source files. Insert the following content into the file and replace `<mongodb-path>` with the location of your MongoDB server:

    ```
    #!/bin/bash
    ls -1 *.json | sed 's/.json$//' | while read col; do case
    "$col" in *_collapsed)
    echo "<mongodb-path>/bin/mongoimport -d foodmart -c sales <
      $col.json;";
    ```

```
<mongodb-path>/bin/mongoimport -d foodmart -c sales <
  $col.json;
;;
esac
echo "<mongodb-path>/bin/mongoimport -d foodmart -c $col <
  $col.json;";
<mongodb-path>/bin/mongoimport -d foodmart -c $col <
  $col.json;
done
```

After some minutes, you will be able to check out the Foodmart data using Mongo shell. After that, perform the following set of instructions:

1. Create a user for the new database. In Mongo shell, execute the following commands:

```
use foodmart;
db.createUser(
{
  user: "root",
  pwd: "password",
  roles: ["readWrite"]
}
);
```

2. Let's enable the `foodmart` connection for the Pentaho native connection:

   1. Go to `http://localhost:8080/pentaho/api/password/encrypt` and submit the password of the MongoDB Foodmart database to get the encrypted password.

      Edit the `<pentaho-installation>/server/biserver-ee/pentaho-solutions/system/olap4j.properties` file and uncomment the lines for the `foodmart` connection, which comes by default. Replace the actual schema file path and MongoDB connection. You should then have something like the following lines:

      ```
      foodmart.name=mongoFoodmart
      foodmart.className=org.pentaho.platform.plugin.services.
      connections.PentahoSystemDriver
      foodmart.connectString=jdbc:mondrian4:Host=localhost;dbname
      =foodmart;DataServicesProvider=com.pentaho.analysis.mongo.Mo
      ngoDataServicesProvider;Catalog=C:/Pentaho/server/biserver-
      ee/pentaho-solutions/system/samples/FoodMart.mongo.xml;usern
      ame=root;password=ENC:cGFzc3dvcmQ
      ```

   2. Restart the Pentaho BI server, and you should be able to use Pentaho Analyzer with the new connection.

How it works...

In previous chapters, we demonstrated how to create MongoDB databases using PDI and how to connect different Pentaho tools to MongoDB. In this particular case, we imported an actual database with good data and used an OLAP schema with different dimensions.

Basically, the `FoodMart.mongo.xml` file is a schema for Mondrian 4, and by using the Olap4j configuration and the Pentaho native connection for MongoDB, it is possible to perform an OLAP analysis directly on top of MongoDB. Internally, the process works like this: the user starts performing an analysis on Mondrian, and the native connection translates Mondrian requests into MongoDB queries using the aggregation framework.

There's more...

There is a tool created by Mark Kromer that helps you create and manage MongoDB connections for Pentaho Analyzer in the olap4j.properties file and Mondrian 4 schema files. You can check out this open source tool, available in the Git repository, by going to `https://github.com/kromerm/MondrianMongoModel`.

Creating a new analysis view using Pentaho Analyzer

Pentaho Analyzer is an analytical visualization tool that filters and drills into data sources. It can easily compile data into visualizations using an interactive web interface and is intuitive for end users. This plugin is available in the Pentaho Enterprise Edition only. If you are using the MongoDB native connection, it is possible to create intuitive and quick visualizations.

This recipe will guide you through exploring the Foodmart data imported in the previous recipe using this analytical tool. This recipe is an overview of the main features available in Pentaho Analyzer.

Getting ready

To get ready for this recipe, you will need the Pentaho BI server running, and make sure you have the MongoDB server running with the data from the previous recipe.

How to do it...

After you have made sure that you are ready to start the recipe, perform the following steps to create an analysis report:

1. From the web browser, access the Pentaho BI server using
   `http://localhost:8080/pentaho`.

2. After logging in, on the **Home** screen, click on the **Create New** button and then on the **Analysis Report** button, as you can see in the following screenshot:

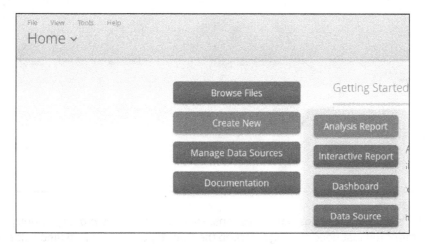

3. In the **Select Data Source** popup, select **mongoFoodmart: Sales**, as you can see in this screenshot:

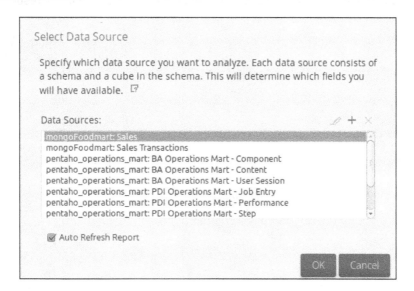

4. You'll get an interactive report with fields in the left-hand-side bar, as you can see in the following screenshot. You can drag and drop, using your mouse, those fields in **Rows**, **Columns**, or indeed **Measures,** if that be the case.

5. Let's answer some business questions, such as *What is my profit by country and state?* You just need to drag and drop the **Country** and **State Province** fields from the **Customers** group to the **Rows** area. You also need to drag and drop the **Profit** field from the **Measures** group to the **Measures** area, and you will instantly get the answer to your business question, as you can see in this screenshot with the result:

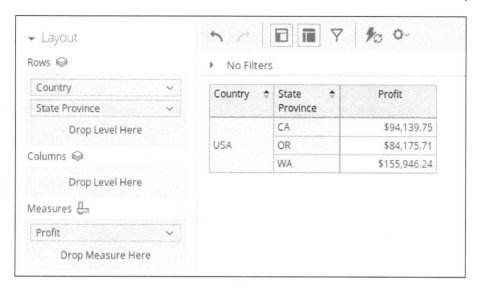

6. Now that we have got the first answer, we can keep asking more questions, such as "What is my profit by country and state for different product families?" Using the same view as earlier, drag and drop the **Product Family** field from the **Products** group to the **Columns** area, and you will quickly get your answer, as shown in the following screenshot:

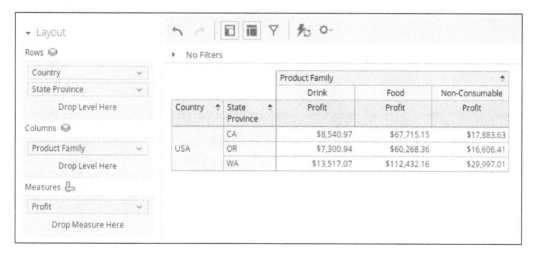

7. Let's answer one more question, *What is my profit by in the cities of California for different product families?* In keeping with the previous view, right-click on the CA state and choose **Keep Only CA**. Then, drag and drop the **City** field from the **Customers** group to the **Rows** area and you will get your answer, as you can see in the following screenshot:

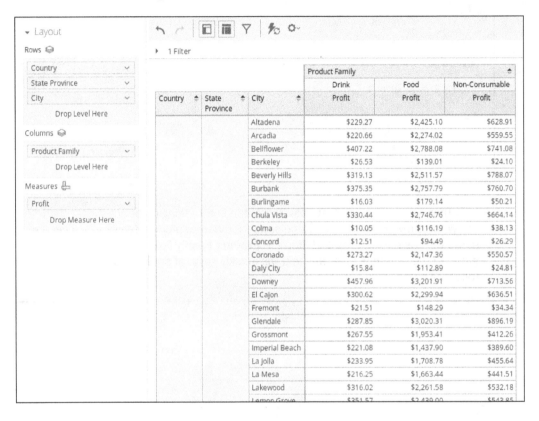

Country	State Province	City	Drink Profit	Food Profit	Non-Consumable Profit
		Altadena	$229.27	$2,425.10	$628.91
		Arcadia	$220.66	$2,274.02	$559.55
		Bellflower	$407.22	$2,788.08	$741.08
		Berkeley	$26.53	$139.01	$24.10
		Beverly Hills	$319.13	$2,511.57	$788.07
		Burbank	$375.35	$2,757.79	$760.70
		Burlingame	$16.03	$179.14	$50.21
		Chula Vista	$330.44	$2,746.76	$664.14
		Colma	$10.05	$116.19	$38.13
		Concord	$12.51	$94.49	$26.29
		Coronado	$273.27	$2,147.36	$550.57
		Daly City	$15.84	$112.89	$24.81
		Downey	$457.96	$3,201.91	$713.56
		El Cajon	$300.62	$2,299.94	$636.51
		Fremont	$21.51	$148.29	$34.34
		Glendale	$287.85	$3,020.31	$896.19
		Grossmont	$267.55	$1,953.41	$412.26
		Imperial Beach	$221.08	$1,437.90	$389.60
		La Jolla	$233.95	$1,708.78	$455.64
		La Mesa	$216.25	$1,663.44	$441.51
		Lakewood	$316.02	$2,261.58	$532.18
		Lemon Grove	$251.57	$2,430.00	$543.85

8. As there are many cities in California, it isn't possible to get any quick understanding of the previous result. Let's convert the table into a stacked column chart in order to get a better understanding. To do this, click on the chart icon in **View As** and choose **Stacked Column**. You will get a quick visualization of your question, as you can see in the next screenshot:

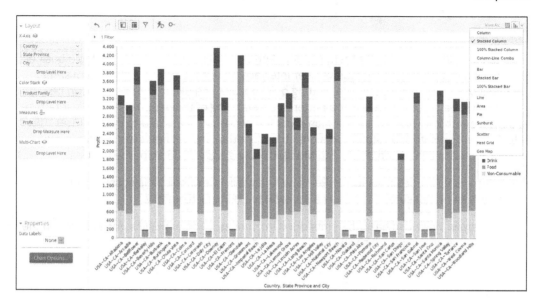

9. Let's save this view by clicking on the **Save** button in the top bar. In the **Save** popup, enter the name `California profit` and save it in your user folder using the `admin` user, as you can see in the following screenshot:

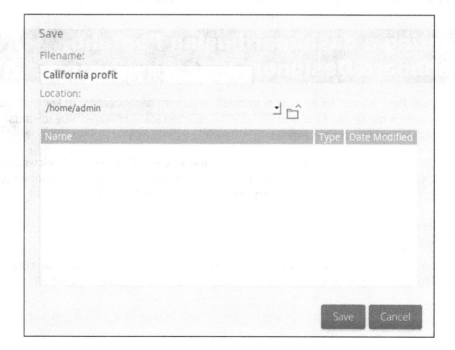

How it works...

With a database and an OLAP schema on top, Pentaho Analyzer can answer multiple business questions quickly and with an intuitive user interface. In this recipe, we just perform some analyses of the Foodmart database, getting quick results in a dynamic table that can be swapped with a proper chart to get a better understanding of the data. This intuitive interface is possible with the OLAP schema, which gives the necessary metadata to the end user. The interface will execute MDX statements onto the Mondrian engine, and then Mondrian will translate the statements on the fly into MongoDB using aggregation pipeline queries.

There are more features available in Pentaho Analyzer; for example, it is possible get the totals by rows or measure columns as a subtotal breaking by hierarchy.

These analysis views can easily be embedded in other systems or plugins; for example, in the next recipe, we will embed this view in a Pentaho dashboard.

There's more...

In the Pentaho marketplace, there is an open source plugin similar to Pentaho Analyzer named **Saiku Analytics**. It's a lightweight JavaScript web interface, and a backend based on web services makes it easier to embed. Saiku also has an enterprise version, just like Pentaho, with extra features that aren't available in the community edition.

Creating a dashboard using Pentaho Dashboard Designer

In these days, having a tool for end users to create their own dashboards with key business indicators using a highly graphical and intuitive visual interface is of huge value towards improving performance in organizations.

Pentaho Dashboard Designer is a plugin that is available only in Pentaho EE. It allows users to easily create their own dashboards. In this recipe guide, you will be able to create a quick and simple dashboard using the Foodmart database storage in MongoDB.

Getting ready

To get ready for this recipe, you will need the Pentaho BI server running, and make sure you have the MongoDB server running with the data from the first recipe of this chapter.

How to do it...

Perform the following steps to create a dashboard:

1. On the **Home** screen, click on the **Create New** button and then on the **Dashboard** button, as you can see in this screenshot:

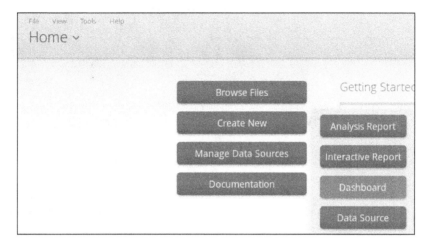

2. In the **Templates** section at the bottom, choose the **1 over 1** option.

3. Under **Properties**, enter the page title as **Dashboard Sample**.

4. In the first panel, click on the insert content dropdown and choose the **File** option, as you can see here:

5. In the **Select** popup, select the `California profit` analysis view file saved in the previous recipe.

6. Set the **Title** field of the panel as **California profit**.

7. In the second panel, import another file. In this case, it is the **Orders Report** file created in the previous chapter.

8. Set the **Title** field of the second panel as **Orders**. You should get a configuration similar to what is shown in this screenshot:

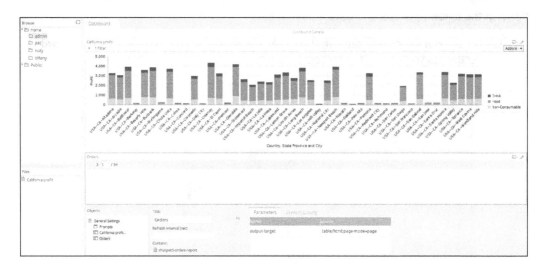

9. Save the dashboard by clicking on the **Save** button in the top bar. In the **Save** popup, enter `Dashboard Sample` in the **Filename** field. Save the dashboard in the same folder as of the previous view and click on **Save**.

10. Now let's open the dashboard in view mode. From the **Home** dropdown, select **Browse Files** and navigate to the repository until you find the dashboard saved earlier. Double-click on the file to open it, and you should see the dashboard as shown in the following screenshot:

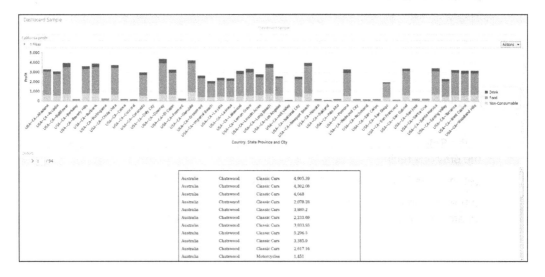

How it works...

This recipe shows you how to create a quick dashboard using an Analyzer view and a Pentaho report created in the previous chapter in two panels. Like Pentaho Analyzer, Pentaho Dashboard Designer is an intuitive plugin for creating your own dashboards quickly, and like Analyzer, Pentaho Dashboard Designer also sends direct MongoDB queries on the fly to the MongoDB cluster. Furthermore, Pentaho Dashboard Designer supports multi-visualization source types such as Pentaho Analyzer, charts, tables, reports, websites, and so on.

There are some more features available on Pentaho Dashboard Designer, such as drill-down and parameters, that help you explore data in the same dashboard.

See also

In the next chapter, we will focus on advanced dashboards using the CDF and CDE community plugins.

7

Pentaho Dashboards

In this chapter, we will cover these recipes:

- ▶ Copying the MongoDB JDBC library
- ▶ Importing a sample repository
- ▶ Using a transformation data source
- ▶ Using a BeanShell data source
- ▶ Using Pentaho Analyzer for MongoDB data source
- ▶ Using a Thin Kettle data source
- ▶ Defining dashboard layouts
- ▶ Creating a Dashboard Table component
- ▶ Creating a Dashboard line chart component

Introduction

These days, we find that giving users an overview of their business in the form of dashboards is one of the most popular forms of reporting solutions. These dashboards give the users a high-level understanding of how their business is performing. From them, the user is likely to further investigate whether their dashboard KPIs are looking good. A dashboard gives users the power to understand their business with minimal time and effort.

In this chapter, you will be able to create advanced and bespoke dashboards using a suite of plugins called **CTools**. CTools is a suite of plugins/components for creating and maintaining advanced dashboards in the Pentaho BI server, available in the Pentaho Marketplace. These can be used in Pentaho Enterprise Edition or even in Pentaho Community Edition. In the more recent Pentaho version, CTools comes preinstalled. However, for the Pentaho EE version, you will need to install the Pentaho Marketplace from `http://community.pentaho.com` and then install the CTools plugins. Based on that, if you follow the procedure in this chapter in Pentaho EE, install Marketplace and CTools before you start the recipes.

Copying the MongoDB JDBC library

We will be using some scripting in these recipes, so it's important to make sure that we have the MongoDB JDBC library copied to the correct location in our Pentaho server.

Getting ready

Make sure you have access to the filesystem that is running your Pentaho server.

How to do it...

Proceed with the following steps:

1. In your filesystem, navigate to `PentahoEE/server/biserver-ee/pentaho-solutions/system/kettle/plugins/pentaho-mongodb-plugin/lib`.
2. Copy the `mongo-java-driver.xxx.jar` file from the folder.
3. Navigate to `PentahoEE/server/biserver-ee/tomcat/webapps/pentaho/WEB-INF/lib`.
4. Paste the `mongo-java-driver.xxx.jar` file.
5. Restart your Pentaho server.

How it works...

By default, it isn't possible to use the scripting/BeanShell data source in dashboards with MongoDB database. This is because the MongoDB Java driver isn't available for the plugin.

In this recipe, we copy the driver that is available in the Kettle BI Server plugin to the `lib` folder of the Pentaho web app. In this way, we can use the MongoDB driver classes in the Pentaho dashboard.

Importing a sample repository

Developing bespoke/advanced dashboards in Pentaho isn't a job for end users. This recipe guides you on how to upload a ZIP file that contains some layouts of dashboards and data sources, so we don't develop dashboards from scratch. This ZIP file, called `Pentaho MongoDB Cookbook.zip`, is available for download along with this book.

You can find more details on the Internet about how to build bespoke dashboards in Pentaho, if you are interesting in learning about them in more detail.

Getting ready

Make sure that your Pentaho BI Server is running and you have logged in to the Pentaho user console.

How to do it...

Proceed with the following steps:

1. In the Pentaho user console, click on **Browse Files**. Then click on the **Public** folder. In the panel to the right, click on the **Upload** button.
2. Next, click on Browse.
3. In your filesystem, navigate to the location of the Pentaho **MongoDB Cookbook.zip** file.
4. Click on **OK**.

How it works...

This recipe guided you through importing a ZIP file that contains a folder with sample resources, which will help you in the upcoming recipes on developing dashboards.

The Pentaho BI Server from version 5.x onward doesn't use the filesystem anymore as a content repository for end users. From this version onward, Pentaho has an implementation of a content repository for Java, providing features of multi-tenancy and content recovery.

Using a transformation data source

Typically, developing dashboards can be useful for getting data from different sources, such as SQL, MDX, APIs, and so on. In cases such as these, it's a good thing to know how to execute a PDI transformation in a dashboard. With PDI transformations, you have almost unlimited power when it comes to data loading and manipulation.

This recipe guides you through creating a PDI transformation data source for a CDE dashboard.

Getting ready

To get ready for this recipe, you first need to start the MongoDB server with the same database as that of the last chapter. You will also need to start the Pentaho BA Server using the server control scripts. Once started, you should be able to log into the BI Server.

How to do it...

Proceed with the following steps:

1. In the **PUC,** go to **File | New | CDE Dashboard**, like this:

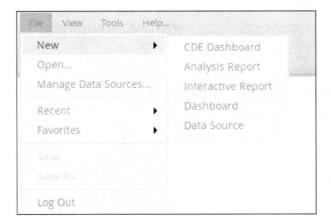

2. Click on the **Data Sources** tab that is shown as selected in the following screenshot:

3. Expand the **KETTLE Queries** data source category.

4. Click on the **Kettle Over KettleFromTransFile** data source, as shown in the following screenshot:

5. Set the **Name** property to **QUERY1**.

6. Click on the **Browse** button on the **Kettle Transformation File** property.

7. Navigate to **Public | Pentaho MongoDB Cookbook | Transformations** and select **Chapter7-getorders.ktr**.

8. Click on **OK**, as shown here:

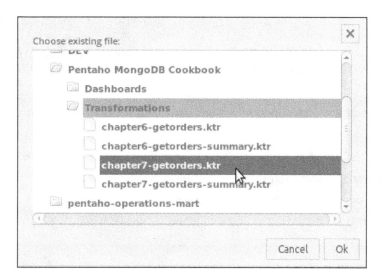

9. Set the **Kettle Step Name** property to **OUT**, like this:

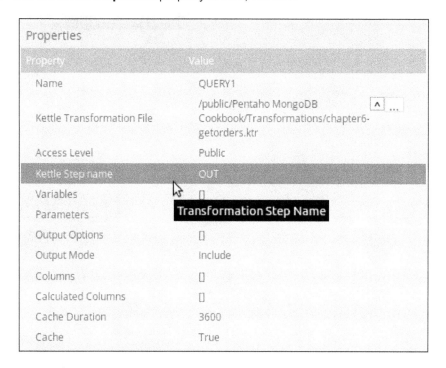

10. Click on **Save As** under the CDE main menu.

11. Save your dashboard in **Public | Pentaho MongoDB Cookbook | Dashboards** with the name `Transformation Data Source`.

In these steps, we simply added a valid data source to the CDE dashboard. However, if we were to preview this dashboard, we wouldn't see any data. This is because we haven't added any dashboard components that use this data source. Instead, the dashboard has saved this connection to another file, called a CDA file. This CDA file is attached to this dashboard and contains all our data sources.

To test that this data source works, we are going to execute it directly from the accompanying CDA file:

1. Click the **Opened** menu on the Pentaho user console and select **Browse Files**.

2. Navigate to **Public | Pentaho MongoDB Cookbook | Dashboards**.

3. Select the **Transformation Data Source.cda** file.

4. Click on **Open** on the right-hand side menu, as shown here:

5. Click on the **Data Access** dropdown and select **Data Access ID: QUERY1**, as shown in the following screenshot:

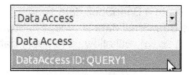

The query will execute once you have selected it from the **Data Access** drop-down menu. You will see the contents of the transformation that is attached to the dashboard you defined earlier, as shown in this screenshot:

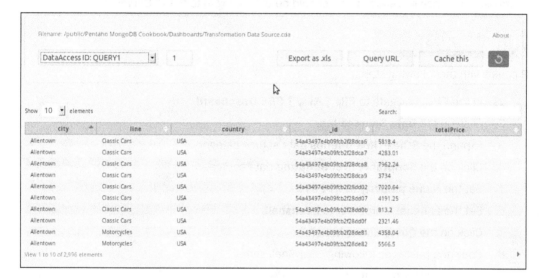

How it works...

In this recipe, we created a new CDE dashboard and added a PDI transformation data source into the data sources section. The data source was added by selecting a transformation that was predefined and saved in the repository when we imported the ZIP file with the sample resources. Once we saved the CDE dashboard, it generated an accompanying CDA file that would store all our data sources.

To test whether the data source was working correctly, we opted to execute the query directly from the generated CDA file. It was possible to see that the transformation was executed successfully in the CDA file and returned a list of orders from the MongoDB database.

Using a BeanShell data source

In this recipe, we are going to create a BeanShell data source, just as we did in previous reporting recipes. This BeanShell data source, a lightweight scripting for Java (http://www.beanshell.org), will allow us to query data from MongoDB.

Getting ready

To get ready for this recipe, you first need to start the MongoDB server with the same database as that of the last chapter. You will also need to start the Pentaho BA Server using the server control scripts. Once it is started, you should be able to log in to the BI Server.

How to do it...

Proceed with the following steps:

1. In the **PUC**, navigate to **File | New | CDE Dashboard**.
2. Click on the **Data Sources** tab.
3. Expand the **SCRIPTING Queries** data source category.
4. Click on the **Scriptable over Scripting** data source.
5. Set the **Name** property to **QUERY2**.
6. Set the **Language** property to **beanshell**.
7. Click on the **Query Editor** button.
8. Copy and paste the following BeanShell script:

```
import com.mongodb.*;
import org.pentaho.reporting.engine.classic.core.util.
TypedTableModel;
Mongo mongo = new Mongo("localhost",27017);
db = mongo.getDB("SteelWheels");
orders = db.getCollection("Orders");
String[] columnNames = {"Country", "City", "Line", "TotalPrice"};
Class[] columnTypes = {String.class, String.class, String.class,
Double.class};
TypedTableModel model = new TypedTableModel(columnNames,
columnTypes);

BasicDBObject dbo = new BasicDBObject();

docs= orders.find(dbo);
```

```
while (docs.hasNext()) {
    doc = docs.next();
  model.addRow(new Object[] {
    doc.get("customer").get("address").get("country"),
    doc.get("customer").get("address").get("city"),
    doc.get("product").get("line"),
    doc.get("totalPrice")
  });
}
docs.close();
return model;
```

The following screenshot displays all the parameters:

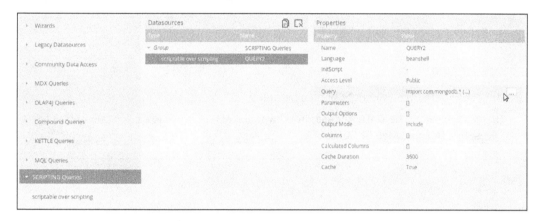

9. Click on **OK**.

10. Click on **Save As** on the CDE main menu.

11. Save your dashboard at **Public | Pentaho MongoDB Cookbook | Dashboards** with the name `Beanshell Data Source`.

To test whether this data source works, we are going to execute the data source directly from the accompanying CDA file:

1. Click on the **Opened** menu on the Pentaho user console and select **Browse Files**.

2. Navigate to **Public | Pentaho MongoDB Cookbook | Dashboards**.

3. Select the **Beanshell Data Source.cda** file.

4. Click on **Open** on the right-hand side menu.

5. Next, click on the **Data Access** dropdown as seen in the following screenshot, and select **Data Access ID : QUERY2**:

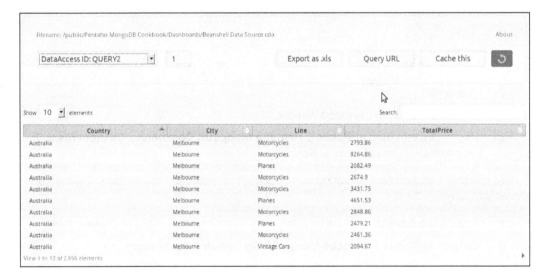

The query will execute once you have selected it from the **Data Access** drop-down menu. You will see the contents of the beanshell query that is attached to the dashboard you defined earlier.

How it works...

In this recipe, we saw how to develop another way of extracting data from MongoDB to the dashboard components, using the MongoDB Java driver and beanshell scripting. We started by creating a new CDE dashboard and adding a BeanShell source to the data sources section. Then, we defined our BeanShell script to return a selection of data directly from MongoDB, using the MongoDB Java driver. Once we had saved the CDE dashboard, it generated an accompanying CDA file that would store all our data sources for the same dashboard. To test that the data source was working correctly, we opted to execute it directly from the generated CDA file. Then, we should be able to see that the beanshell scripts are executed successfully in the CDA file and return a list of orders from the MongoDB database.

Using Pentaho Analyzer for MongoDB data source

In this recipe, we are going to connect to our MongoDB database using an MDX query from Pentaho Analyzer. We are going to create a simple query using Analyzer, copy the generated MDX, and create a data source in CDE to execute the MDX query.

Getting ready

To get ready for this recipe, you first need to start the MongoDB server with the same database as that in the last chapter. You will also have to start the Pentaho BA Server using the server control scripts. Once it is started, you can log in to the BI Server.

How to do it...

The first step is to create an MDX query using the Pentaho EE Analyzer:

1. In the **PUC**, navigate to **File | New | Analysis Report**.

2. Select the **mongoDBPentahoCookBook: Orders** data source from the list of available data sources, like this:

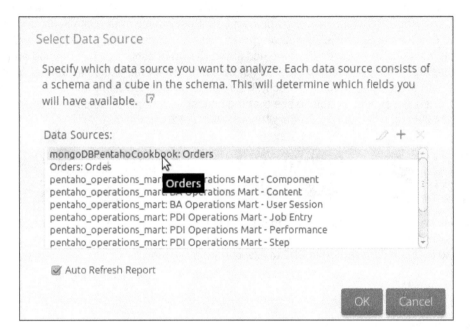

3. Click on **OK**.

4. Click and drag the **Country** field from the **Customers** dimension to the analysis report canvas.

5. Then, click and drag **Total Price** from the **Measures** dimension to the analysis report canvas next to **Country**, as shown here:

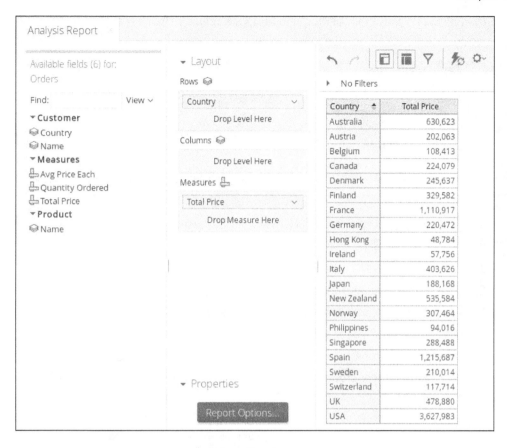

6. Click on the **cog icon** on the **Analyzer** toolbar.

7. Go to **Administration | Log**. This will open a new browser tab.

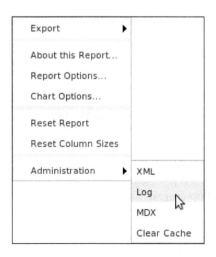

8. Select and copy the MDX from the **Message** column. Make sure you select only the MDX query, as shown in this screenshot:

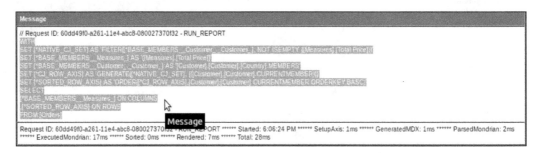

We now have an MDX query that we can add to our CDE Dashboard. Let's create the dashboard and add this MDX as a data source:

1. In the PUC, go to **File | New | CDE Dashboard**.

2. Click on the **Data Sources** tab.

3. Expand the OLAP4J Queries data source category.

4. Click on the **olap4j over olap4j** data source.

5. Set the **Name** property to **QUERY3**.

6. Then set the **Driver** property to `org.pentaho.platform.plugin.services.connections.PentahoSystemDriver`.

7. Next, set the **URL** property to the following:

   ```
   jdbc:mondrian4:Host=localhost;dbname=SteelWheels;DataServicesPro
   vider=com.pentaho.analysis.mongo.MongoDataServicesProvider;Catal
   og=/home/latino/git/pentaho-mongodb-cookbook/source code/chapter4/
   MongoDBPentahoCookbook.mondrian.xml.
   ```

8. Open the **Query Editor** property, and copy and paste the following MDX query:

   ```
   WITH

   SET [*NATIVE_CJ_SET] AS 'FILTER([*BASE_MEMBERS__Customer_._
   Customer_], NOT ISEMPTY ([Measures].[Total Price]))'

   SET [*BASE_MEMBERS__Measures_] AS '{[Measures].[Total Price]}'

   SET [*BASE_MEMBERS__Customer_._Customer_] AS '[Customer].
   [Customer].[Country].MEMBERS'

   SET [*CJ_ROW_AXIS] AS 'GENERATE([*NATIVE_CJ_SET], {([Customer].
   [Customer].CURRENTMEMBER)})'

   SET [*SORTED_ROW_AXIS] AS 'ORDER([*CJ_ROW_AXIS],[Customer].
   [Customer].CURRENTMEMBER.ORDERKEY,BASC)'
   ```

```
SELECT
[*BASE_MEMBERS__Measures_] ON COLUMNS
,[*SORTED_ROW_AXIS] ON ROWS
FROM [Orders]
```

This is the query you generated in the **Analyzer** report in previous steps.

9. Click on **OK**.

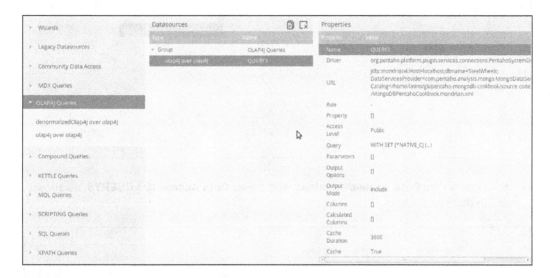

10. Click on **Save As** in the CDE Main Menu.
11. Save your dashboard by going to **Public | Pentaho MongoDB Cookbook |
    Dashboards**, with the name MongOLAP Data Source.

To test whether this data source works, we are going to execute it directly from the
accompanying CDA file:

1. Click on the **Opened** menu on the Pentaho User Console and select **Browse Files**.
2. Navigate to **Public | Pentaho MongoDB Cookbook | Dashboards**.
3. Select the **MongOLAP Data Source.cda** file, as shown in the next screenshot.

4. Click on **Open** on the right-hand side menu.

5. Click on the **Data Access** dropdown and select **Data Access ID : QUERY3**, as shown in this screenshot:

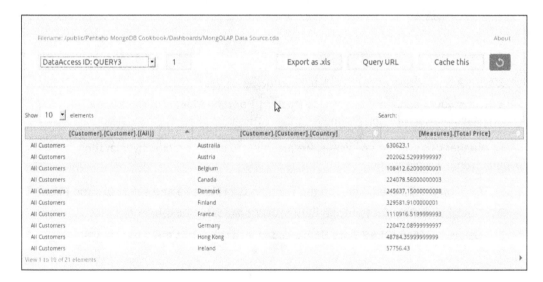

The query will execute once you have selected it from the **Data Access** drop-down menu. You will see the contents of the MDX query that is attached to the dashboard you defined earlier.

How it works...

In this recipe, we guided you through using Pentaho Analyzer to generate an MDX query that you can use on a dashboard. In dashboard editor mode, you will need to add a custom OLAP4J data source, set the driver connection URL, and set the MDX query copied from Pentaho Analyzer. After saving the dashboard, we can execute the query from the CDA file and see the results from the cube.

This is another way of using MongoDB connectivity—by using analysis cubes. However, this type of connectivity is available in the Pentaho EE version only, as Pentaho Analyzer is an enterprise plugin.

Using a Thin Kettle data source

In this recipe, we are going to execute a SQL query that will be passed down to the Thin Kettle driver. This special driver will convert the standard SQL query into something that MongoDB can understand. The Thin Kettle driver allows users to execute standard SQL against MongoDB.

Getting ready

To get ready for this recipe, you first need to start the MongoDB server with the same database as that of the last chapter. You will also have to start the Pentaho BA Server using the server control scripts. Once it is started, you can log in to the BI Server.

How to do it...

Perform the following steps:

1. In the **PUC**, go to **File | New | CDE Dashboard**.
2. Click on the **Data Sources** tab.
3. Expand the **SQL Queries** data source category.
4. Click on the **sql over sqljndi** data source.
5. Set the **Name** property to **QUERY4**.
6. Then set the **JNDI** property to **Pentaho MongoDB Cookbook Kettle Thin**.

7. Open the **Query Editor** property, and copy and paste the following SQL query:

```
select customerCountry, SUM(totalPrice) as totalSales
from Orders
group by customerCountry
```

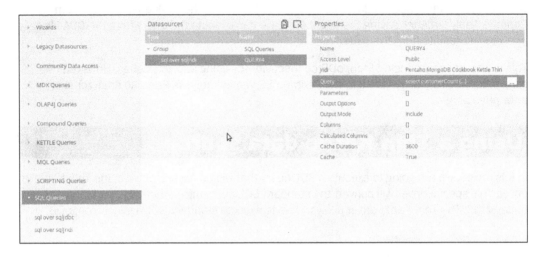

8. Click on Save As under the CDE Main Menu.

9. Save your dashboard at **Public | Pentaho MongoDB Cookbook | Dashboards**, with the name **Kettle Thin Data Source**.

To verify that this data source works, we are going to execute it directly from the accompanying CDA file:

1. Click on the **Opened** menu on the **Pentaho User Console** and select **Browse Files**.

2. Navigate to **Public | Pentaho MongoDB Cookbook | Dashboards**.

3. Select the **Kettle Thin Data Source.cda** file, as shown in the next screenshot:

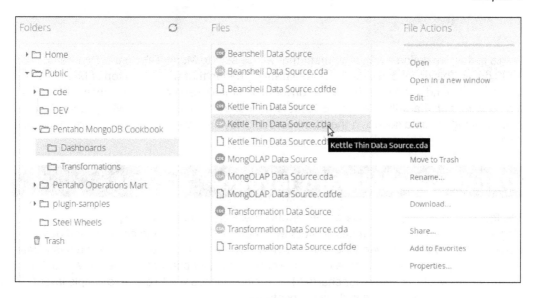

4. Click on **Open** from the right-hand side menu.

5. Click on the **Data Access** dropdown and select **Data Access ID : QUERY4**.

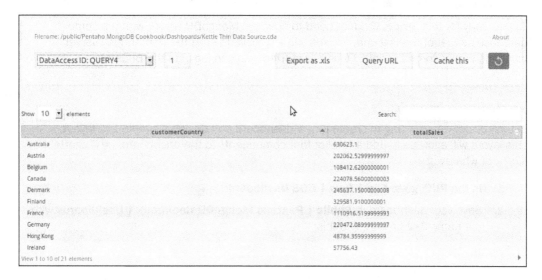

The query will execute once you have selected it from the Data Access drop-down menu. You will see the contents of the SQL query that is attached to the dashboard that you defined earlier.

How it works...

In this recipe, we define a SQL statement that will be sent to MongoDB via the Thin Kettle JDBC driver. This driver converts SQL into a transformation that will run on top of MongoDB. In the background, the Kettle Thin JDBC driver (using the DI server or Carte server) generates a transformation that will take in an SQL statement and get data from the MongoDB database. After defining the data source in the dashboard and saving it, we're able to test this connection by running the data source in the CDA file.

Defining dashboard layouts

The foundation of every dashboard is its layout. These can range from simple layouts with a single chart to much more complex layouts with many nested rows and columns and many different-sized charts, or even other components such as filters. When we create a dashboard, we usually define the layout before we define data sources or chart components. Without a layout, where would we place our charts? This recipe teaches you to create a simple layout using a responsive web framework called bootstrap.

Getting ready

To get ready for this recipe, you first need to start the MongoDB server with the same database as that of the last chapter. You will also have to start the Pentaho BA Server using the server control scripts. Once it is started, you can log in to the BI Server.

How to do it...

In this recipe, we are going to create a new dashboard and design a simple 2x2 layout. This layout will allow us to add a total of four components to the dashboard, be it charts, filters, or whatever:

1. In the **PUC**, go to **File | New | CDE Dashboard**.
2. Save your dashboard in **Public | Pentaho MongoDB Cookbook | Dashboards** with the name **2x2 Layout**, like this:

3. Click on **Settings** on the **CDE Main Menu**.

4. Set Dashboard Type to bootstrap, as shown here:

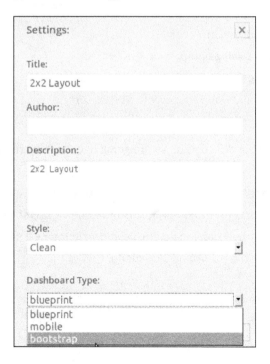

5. Click on the **Layout** tab.

6. Then click on the **Add Row** button.

7. Select the row.

8. Click on the **Add Column** button.

9. Make sure that the row is still selected.

10. Click on the **Add Column** button again.

11. Select the first nested column.

12. Set the **Medium Devices** property to **6**.

13. Then set the **Height** property to **300**.

14. Next, set the **Background Color** property to **#CCCCCC**.

15. Select the second column.

16. Set the **Medium Devices** property to **6**.

17. Then set the **Height** property to 300.

18. Set the **Background Color** property to **#BBBBBB**.

19. Click on Save.

Now that we have saved our dashboard, we are going to open it in render mode to see what it looks like:

1. Click on the **Opened** menu on the **Pentaho User Console** and select **Browse Files**.

2. Navigate to **Public | Pentaho MongoDB Cookbook | Dashboards**.

3. Select the **2x2 Layout** dashboard file, as shown in the next screenshot.

4. Click on **Open** on the right-hand side menu.

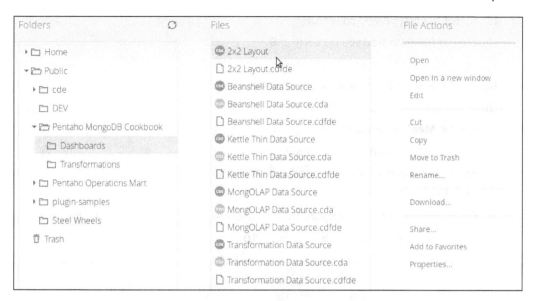

You can see that we have created a simple two-column layout. We could technically start adding dashboard components such as charts and filters to these two areas. But, let's go back to the original dashboard we were editing and add some more layout.

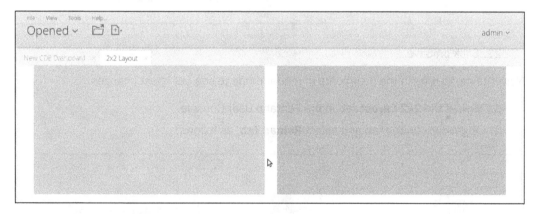

5. Select the original row with the two nested columns.

6. Click on the **Add Row** button to add a new row to the layout. This new row will appear below the original row in the root of the dashboard structure.

7. Select the new row.

8. Click on the **Add Column** button.

9. Make sure that the row is still selected.

10. Click on the **Add Column** button again.

11. Select the first nested column.

12. Set the **Medium Devices** property to **6**.

13. Then set the **Height** property to **300**.

14. Set the **Background Color** property to **#CCCCCC**.

15. Select the second column.

16. Set the **Medium Devices** property to **6**.

17. Next, set the **Height** property to 300.

18. Set the **Background Color** property to **#BBBBBB**.

19. Select the **first** row.

20. Click on the **Add Spacer** button. This will add a small space between the two rows.

21. Set the **Height** property of the spacer to **10.**

22. Click on Save.

Now it's time to refresh the dashboard in render mode to see our latest changes.

1. Select the **2x2 Layout** tab in the Pentaho User Console.

2. Right-click on the tab and select **Reload Tab**, as follows:

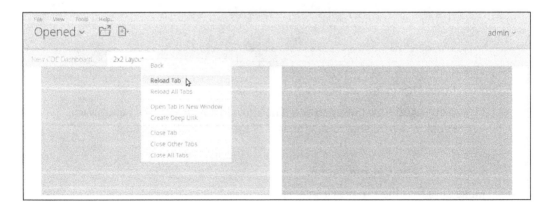

You will now see a simple 2x2 layout with four main panels, like this:

To finish off, we will add a simple HTML component to the top-left layout column.

3. Select the first column in the first row of the dashboard is layout structure.

4. Click on the **Add HTML** button.

5. Open the **HTML Editor** property.

6. Copy and paste the following **HTML**:

   ```
   <h2 style="margin-top:0px">My Dashboard</h2>
   ```

7. Click on **OK**. The following screenshot shows the Layout Structure window:

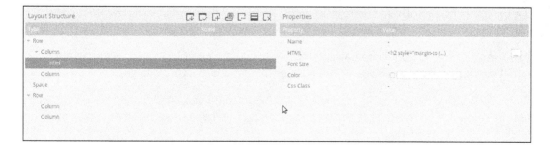

8. Then click on **Save**.

Let's refresh our latest changes on the dashboard:

1. Select the **2x2 Layout** tab in the Pentaho User Console.

2. Right-click on the tab and select **Reload Tab**.

    You can see that we have added some basic HTML to our dashboard, as follows:

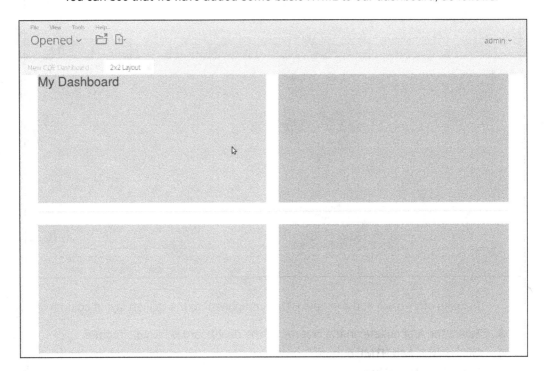

How it works...

In this recipe, we showed you how to create a new dashboard and define a layout of rows and nested columns. It's possible to nest further rows into columns and more columns into those rows. It is even possible to set the size of columns that add up to a total value of 12 based on the bootstrap framework. To create a 50 on 50 layout, we set each column to a width of 6. We could have also created a layout with four columns, each having a width of 3.

Plus, we were able to add some basic HTML to our layout. The ability to add HTML to our layout opens the door to all sorts of possibilities in dashboard layout design.

Basically, by using the bootstrap framework, CDE, and some imagination, it is possible create bespoke responsive dashboards that will fit in different screens types, such as desktops, tablets, or mobile phones.

Creating a Dashboard Table component

In this recipe, we are going to add a Table component to a dashboard so that we can render a data source result for the user.

Getting ready

To get ready for this recipe, you first need to start the MongoDB server with the same database as that of the last chapter. You will also need to start the Pentaho BA Server using the server control scripts. Once it is started, you should be able to log in to the BI Server.

How to do it...

Proceed with the following steps:

1. In the **PUC**, go to **File | New | CDE Dashboard**.
2. Save your dashboard in **Public | Pentaho MongoDB Cookbook | Dashboards** with the name **Table Component**.
3. Click on **Settings** in the **CDE Main Menu**.
4. Click on the **Layout** tab.
5. Then click on the **Add Row** button.
6. Select **Row**.
7. Set the **Name** property to **ROW1**.
8. Then set the **Height** property to **300**, as shown here:

9. Click on the **Data Sources** tab.
10. Expand the **KETTLE Queries** data source category.
11. Click on the **kettle over kettleTransFromFile** data source.
12. Set the **Name** property to **QUERY1**.
13. Click on the **Browse** button on the **Kettle Transformation File** property.
14. Navigate to **Public | Pentaho MongoDB Cookbook | Transformations**.

15. Select **Chapter7-getorders.ktr**.

16. Click on **OK**.

17. Set the **Kettle Step name** property to **OUT**, like this:

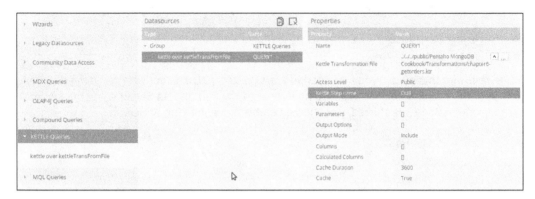

18. Click on the **Component** tab.

19. Expand the **Others** category.

20. Add a **Table Component**.

21. Set the **Name** property to **TABLE1**.

22. Then set the **Datasource** property to **QUERY1**.

23. Next, set the **HTML Object** property to **ROW1**, as follows:

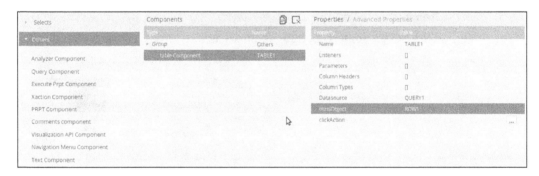

24. Click on **Save**.

We can now preview our dashboard as follows:

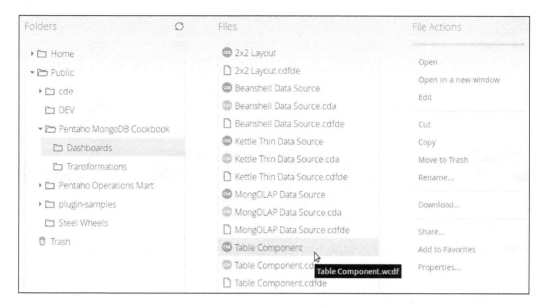

1. Click on the **Opened** menu on the Pentaho User Console and select **Browse Files**.

2. Navigate to **Public | Pentaho MongoDB Cookbook | Dashboards**.

3. Select the **Table Component** dashboard file.

4. Click on **Opened** on the right-hand side menu and the following screenshot should appear:

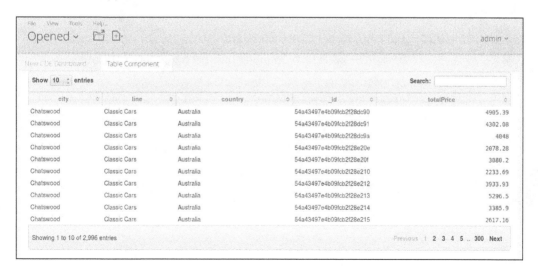

How it works...

In this recipe, we created a simple but functional dashboard. After we had created an empty dashboard, we created a data source based on a Pentaho Transformation. Finally, we added a Table component to the dashboard, hooked it up with the **QUERY1** data source, and placed it on a layout row called **ROW1**.

These are the basics you need for 99% of your dashboards. You need a layout, data sources, and components that execute the data sources and render the results on the dashboard layout.

Creating a Dashboard line chart component

In this recipe, we are going to add a line chart component to a dashboard. Charts play an important role in dashboard design. There are all sorts of chart components available in the CDE Dashboard editor, but we are only going to cover the line chart component. You will notice that many of the charts out here have the same options (not all options, but some).

Getting ready

To get ready for this recipe, you first need to start the MongoDB server with the same database as that of the last chapter. You will also need to start the Pentaho BA Server using the server control scripts. Once it is started, you should be able to log in to the BI Server.

How to do it...

Proceed with the following steps:

1. In the **PUC**, go to **File | New | CDE Dashboard**.
2. Save your dashboard at **Public | Pentaho MongoDB Cookbook | Dashboards**, with the name `Line Chart Component`.
3. Click on **Settings** on the **CDE Main Menu**.
4. Click on the **Layout** tab.
5. Then click on the **Add Row** button.
6. Select **Row**.
7. Set the **Name** property to **ROW1**.
8. Set the **Height** property to **300**.
9. Click on the **Data Sources** tab.

10. Expand the **Kettle Queries** data source category.

11. Click on the **Kettle Over kettleTransFromFile** data source.

12. Set the **Name** property to **QUERY1**.

13. Click on the **Browse** button of the **Kettle Transformation File** property.

14. Navigate to **Public | Pentaho MongoDB Cookbook | Transformations**.

15. Select **Chapter7-getorders-summary.ktr**.

16. Click on **OK**.

17. Set the **Kettle Step name** property to **OUT**, like this:

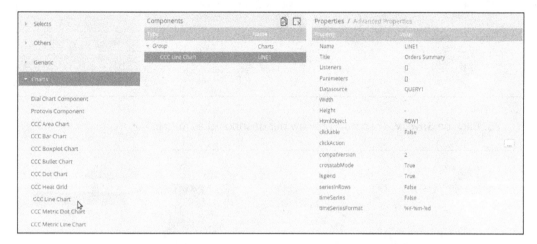

18. Click on the **Component** tab.

19. Expand the **Charts** category.

20. Add **CCC Line Chart**.

21. Set the **Name** property to **LINE1**.

22. Then set the **Title** property to **Orders Summary**.

23. Next, set the **Datasource** property to **QUERY1**.

24. Finally, set the **HTML Object** property to **ROW1**. The following screenshot should appear:

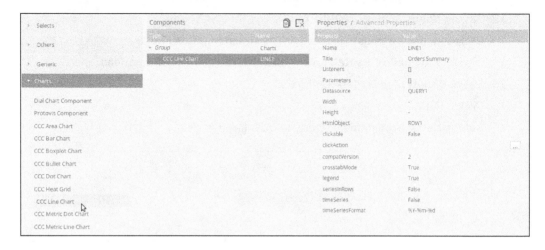

25. Click on **Save**. We can now preview our dashboard as follows:

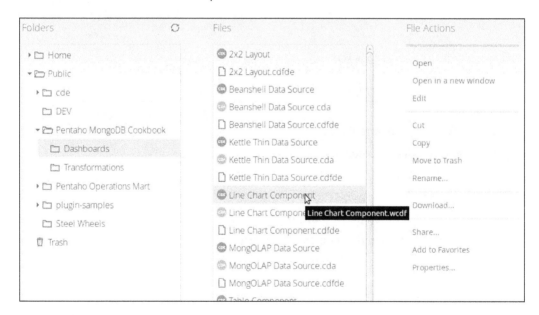

26. Click on the **Opened** menu on the Pentaho User Console and select **Browse Files**.

27. Navigate to **Public | Pentaho MongoDB Cookbook | Dashboards**.

28. Select the **Line Chart Component** dashboard file.

29. Click on **Opened** on the left-hand side menu.

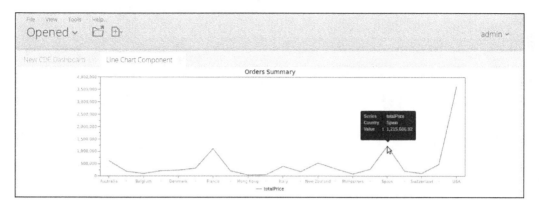

How it works...

In this recipe, we created a simple but functional dashboard. After creating an empty dashboard, we created a data source based on a Pentaho transformation. We finally added a line chart component to the dashboard, hooked it up with the **QUERY1** data source, and placed it on a layout row called **ROW1**.

8
Pentaho Community Contributions

In this chapter, we will cover these recipes:

- ▶ The PDI MongoDB Delete step
- ▶ The PDI MongoDB GridFS Output step
- ▶ The PDI MongoDB Map/Reduce Output step
- ▶ The PDI MongoDB Lookup step

Introduction

Pentaho Data Integration and the Pentaho BI server include a Marketplace plugin, where the community (individual users/developers or companies) can submit plugins to everyone so that they can use it.

This chapter focuses on PDI plugins related to MongoDB developed by the Pentaho community. By default, Pentaho supports MongoDB, as was demonstrated in the first chapter. However, there is much more functionality from MongoDB that is a gap in Pentaho Enterprise. Pentaho Data Integration with a great pluggable architecture and a good open source ecosystem allows developers to contribute new steps and features. Because of this, some community members have already closed some gaps with some open source solutions available in the Marketplace. Without these features, you'll need to develop Java code at the **User Defined Class** step, or develop your own custom step to support the features.

This chapter focuses on PDI contributions. However, this doesn't mean that there doesn't exist good plugins for the Pentaho BI server. There are good plugins such as Saiku Analytics. Anyway! The Pentaho BI server is a web platform focused on administration and visualizations, and PDI is responsible for manipulating the data in the first layer of interaction with MongoDB in most cases.

The PDI MongoDB Delete Step

In this recipe, we will cover the functionality of the MongoDB Delete step. This step was developed by Maas Dianto and is open source under the Apache License version 2.0. It is available on GitHub at `https://github.com/maasdi/pentaho-mongodb-delete-plugin`.

As the name suggests, this step deletes documents from a collection based on conditions defined by the user.

Getting ready

To get ready for this recipe, you will need to start your ETL development environment **Spoon**, and make sure that you have the MongoDB server running with the data from the previous chapters.

How to do it...

Let's install and use the MongoDB Delete step in a small example by following the next steps:

1. Now let's install the MongoDB Delete step:
    1. On the menu bar of Spoon, select **Help** and then **Marketplace**.
    2. A **PDI Marketplace** popup will show you the list of plugins available for installation. Search for **MongoDB** in the **Detected Plugins** field.
    3. Expand the **MongoDB Delete Plugin** item, as you can see in the following screenshot:

```
▽ ¾ MongoDB Delete Plugin - not installed
                 ID: pentaho-mongodb-delete-plugin
               Name: MongoDB Delete Plugin
     Available version: 1.0.0-RELEASE
            Authors: Maas Dianto
Plugin installation path: /home/latino/Documents/pentaho-ee/design-tools/data-integration/plugins/steps
         Description: Delete document inside a MongoDB collection
        Package URL: https://github.com/maasdi/pentaho-mongodb-delete-plugin/releases/download/1.0.0-RELEASE/pentaho-mongodb-delete-
                     plugin-1.0.0-RELEASE.zip
       Documentation: https://github.com/maasdi/pentaho-mongodb-delete-plugin/wiki/MongoDB-Delete
        Case Tracking: https://github.com/maasdi/pentaho-mongodb-delete-plugin/issues
            License: Apache License 2.0
     License Details: For more details see:
                     http://www.apache.org/licenses/LICENSE-2.0.html

       Support Level: Community Supported

                     [ Install this plugin ]
```

4. Click on the **Install this plugin** button.

5. Next, click on the **OK** button in the alert for restarting Spoon.

6. Restart Spoon.

2. Let's delete the order of the **Baane Mini Imports** customer with **priceEach** more than or equal to **100**:

   1. Using the MongoDB shell, check how many documents exist. Upon running the following query, you should get 20 as the result:

      ```
      db.Orders.find({"priceEach":{$gte:100},"customer.name":
      "Baane Mini Imports"}).count()
      ```

   2. In Spoon, create a new transformation with the name `delete-mongodb-documents.ktr`.

   3. Select the **Design** tab in the left-hand-side view.

   4. From the **Input** category folder, find the **Generate Rows** step and drag and drop it into the working area in the right-hand side view.

   5. Double-click on the step to open the **Generate Rows** configuration dialog.

   6. Set **Step Name** to **Get Values**.

   7. Set the **Limit** field to **1**.

   8. In the **Fields** table, add the `customerName` field as a `String` type with the value `Baane Mini Imports`. In a new row, add the `priceEach` field as a **Number** type with the value **100**.

   9. In the **Big Data** category folder, find the **MongoDB Delete** step and drag and drop it into the working area in the right-hand-side view.

   10. Connect the **Get Values** step to the **MongoDB Delete** step.

11. Double-click on the step to open the **MongoDB Delete** configuration dialog.

12. Select the **Delete options** tab, click on the **Get Dbs** button, and select **SteelWheels** from the **Database** field. Then, click on the **Get collections** button and select **Orders** from the **Collection** field.

13. Select the **Delete Query** tab. In the **Mongo document path** field, add the **priceEach** and **customer.name** fields. The **Comparator** field for **priceEach** is **>=**, and for **customer.name**, it is **=**. In **incoming field 1**, set **priceEach** and **customerName**, as you can see in this screenshot:

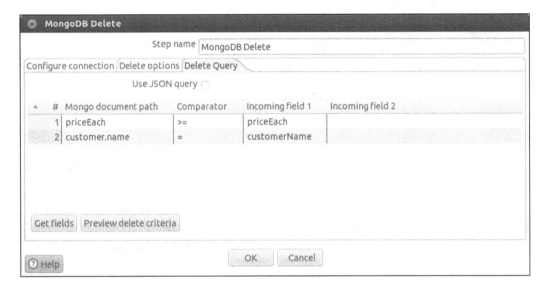

14. Finally, run the transformation with a structure like what is shown in the following screenshot:

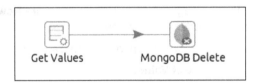

15. If you run the same query that was executed before, you should get **0** as the result.

How it works...

In this recipe, using the MongoDB Delete step, we delete from the `SteelWheels` database all the documents in the **Orders** collection that have the **Baane Mini Imports** customer name and whose **priceEach** value is more than or equal to **100**. We use the **Generate Rows** step just to create one row, for testing purposes.

However, PDI gives you the flexibility to read data from different data sources and then apply the rules that you need. For example, you can read customer names from a hypersonic database and then delete them from a MongoDB database. This is a good exercise for you to try.

The PDI MongoDB GridFS Output Step

The BJSON document size in MongoDB is limited to 16 MB. If you want to store large files and/or different file types, you can use GridFS. There are some cases in which storing large files may be more efficient in MongoDB than in a filesystem, for example, if the filesystem is limited in the number of files in a directory or it's possible to access only some portions of large files without loads all the files in the memory.

SPEC INDIA has contributed to the Pentaho community with the MongoDB GridFS Output Step under a GPL license on GitHub at `https://github.com/SPECUSA/MongoDBGridfs`.

Getting ready

To get ready for this recipe, you will again need to start your ETL development environment Spoon and make sure that you have the MongoDB server running with the data from the previous chapters.

How to do it...

Perform the following steps to use the MongoDB GridFS Output step:

1. Let's install the MongoDB GridFS Output step:
    1. From the menu bar of Spoon, select **Help** and then **Marketplace**.
    2. A **PDI Marketplace** popup will show you the list of plugins available for installation. Search for **MongoDB** in the **Detected Plugins** field.

3. Expand the **MongoDB GridFS Output Plugin** item, as you can see in the following screenshot:

4. Click on the **Install this plugin** button.

5. Next, click on the **OK** button in the alert for restarting Spoon.

6. Restart Spoon.

2. Let's insert the `orders.csv` file. This file is available in the source code of this chapter, in the MongoDB `files` database:

1. In Spoon, create a new transformation with the name `insert-order.csv-mongodb.ktr`.

2. Select the **Design** tab in the left-hand-side view.

3. From the **Input** category folder, find the **Generate Rows** step, and drag and drop it into the working area in the right-hand-side view.

4. Double-click on the step to open the **Generate Rows** configuration dialog.

5. Set **Step Name** to **Get order.csv**.

6. Set the **Limit** field to **1**.

7. In the **Fields** table, add the **filePath** field as a **String** type and set the value with the location of the **order.csv** source file in your filesystem.

8. From the **Big Data** category folder, find the **Mongodb GridFS Output** step, and drag and drop it into the working area in the right-hand-side view.

9. Connect the **Get Values** step to the **Mongodb GridFS Output** step.

10. Double-click on the step to open the **Mongodb GridFS Output** configuration dialog.

11. Set **Step Name** to **Insert order.csv**.

12. Next, set the **Database** field to **files** and the **GridFS Bucket** field to **fileBucket**.

13. In the **File** field, select the **filePath** option. The configuration should look like what is shown in this screenshot:

14. Click on the **OK** button.

15. You will be able to run the transformation successfully. After that, you can, using the MongoDB shell, check whether a new database called `files` exists. To check whether the file was inserted, you can run the following query:

```
db.fileBucket.files.find().pretty();
```

16. Then see the information about the new file. The transformation should look like what is shown here:

How it works...

Basically, this recipe guides you through inserting a file into GridFS of MongoDB. However, you can insert any other file, and as many as you wish.

Storing entire files in MongoDB isn't a usual operation to do, but in some cases, it may be a good option for getting dynamic storage space with shards and replication.

A good exercise, if you understand the functionality of GridFS, is to create a transformation that gets the list of all the files available in a particular folder of your filesystem, and insert them into MongoDB.

The PDI MongoDB Map/Reduce Output step

Most aggregation operations in MongoDB are done by the Aggregation Framework, which provides better performance, but in some cases, it is necessary that it possesses flexibility that isn't present in it and is just possible with Map/Reduce commands.

Ivy Information Systems has contributed a plugin with two MongoDB steps—MongoDB Map/Reduce and MongoDB Lookup—under the AGPL license. These are available on GitHub at `https://github.com/ivylabs/ivy-pdi-mongodb-steps`.

Getting ready

To get ready for this recipe, you will need to start your ETL development environment Spoon, and make sure that you have the MongoDB server running with the data from the previous chapters.

How to do it...

Perform the following steps to create a quick sample for users with MongoDB Map/Reduce in PDI:

1. Let's install the Ivy PDI MongoDB by performing the following steps:

    1. On the menu bar of Spoon, select **Help** and then **Marketplace**.

    2. A **PDI Marketplace** popup will show you the list of plugins available for installation. Search for `MongoDB` in the **Detected Plugins** field.

3. Expand the **Ivy PDI MongoDB Steps** Plugin item. As you can see in the following screenshot:

▼ ⚡ Ivy PDI MongoDB Steps - not installed

ID:	IvyMongoDBSteps
Name:	Ivy PDI MongoDB Steps
Available version:	1.0.0
Min. PDI version:	5.0
Authors:	Ivy Information Systems Ltd.
Plugin installation path:	/home/latino/Documents/pentaho-ee/design-tools/data-integration/plugins/steps
Description:	Pentaho data integration plugin for MongoDB.
Package URL:	http://sourceforge.net/projects/ivylabs/files/Pentaho/Data%20Integration/PDI%20MongoDB%20Steps/1.0.0/IvyMongoDBSteps.zip/download
Documentation:	https://github.com/ivylabs/ivy-pdi-mongodb-steps/blob/master/README.md
Source Code:	https://github.com/ivylabs/ivy-pdi-mongodb-steps/tree/1.0.0
License:	AGPL
License Details:	For more details see: https://www.gnu.org/licenses/agpl-3.0.html
Support Level:	Community Supported
Support Message:	Supported by Ivy Information Systems Ltd.
Support URL:	http://www.ivy-is.co.uk/contact-us/

Install this plugin

4. Click on the **Install this plugin** button.

5. Next, click on the **OK** button in the alert for restarting Spoon.

6. Restart Spoon.

2. Let's make the same Map/Reduce transformation that was made in the first chapter with **User Defined Java Class** to prove how much easier it is:

1. In Spoon, create a new transformation with the name `mongodb-map-reduce.ktr`.

2. Under the **Transformation properties** and **Parameters** tab, create a new parameter with the **CUSTOMER_NAME** name.

3. Select the **Design** tab in the left-hand-side view.

4. From the **Big Data** category folder, find the **MongoDB Map/Reduce Input** step, and drag and drop it into the working area in the right-hand-side view.

5. Double-click on the step to open the **MongoDB Map/Reduce Input** configuration dialog.

6. Set **Step Name** to **Get data**.

7. In the **Configure connection** tab, click on the **Get DBs** button and select the **SteelWheels** option for the **Database** field. Then, click on the **Get collections** button and select the **Orders** option for the **Collection** field.

8. In the **Map function** tab, set this JavaScript map function:

```
function() {
  var category;
  if ( this.customer.name == '${CUSTOMER_NAME}' )
    category = '${CUSTOMER_NAME}';
  else
    category = 'Others';
  emit(category, {totalPrice: this.totalPrice, count: 1});
}
```

9. In the **Reduce function** tab, set the following JavaScript reduce function:

```
function(key, values) {
  var n = { count: 0, totalPrice: 0};
  for ( var i = 0; i < values.length; i++ ) {
    n.count += values[i].count;
    n.totalPrice += values[i].totalPrice;
  }
  return n;
}
```

10. Then, in the **Fields** tab, click on the **Get fields** button, and you'll be able to get new fields there: **_id**, **count**, and **totalPrice**. Remove the **_id** field. The final configuration should look like this:

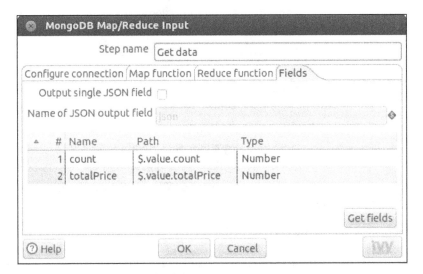

11. Click on the **OK** button.

12. From the **Flow** category folder, find the **Dummy (do nothing)** step, and drag and drop it into the working area in the right-hand-side view.

13. Connect the **Get data** step to the **Dummy (do nothing)** step.

14. Double-click on the step to open the **Dummy (do nothing)** configuration dialog.

15. Set **Step Name** to **OUT**.

16. Click on the **OK** button. The transformation should be similar to what is shown in the following screenshot, and you may be able to preview the execution transformation:

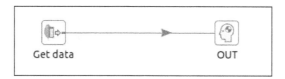

How it works...

Using this step for Map and Reduce is much easier than using the UJDC step, but the latter is much flexible in the way for processing data; however, users are prone to making mistakes.

The Map and Reduce functions in MongoDB are in JavaScript, and you can get more flexibility because the map function can create more than one key and value mapping or no mapping at all.

This recipe was a simple example based on the last recipe of the first chapter, but using this popular data processing paradigm, you can perform many complex queries as you like.

See also

In the *MongoDB Map/Reduce using the User Defined Java Class step* and *MongoDB Java Driver* recipe of the first chapter, we have explained the same functionality, but using the User Defined Java Class step.

The PDI MongoDB Lookup step

As you know, it isn't possible to join different collections in MongoDB as it is in a typical relational database. Sometimes, this functionality is necessary and needs to be applied in other layers of your system. This is a gap in Pentaho Data Integration, and it was solved in a particular way by Ivy Information Systems in the same plugin that is mentioned in the previous recipe with the MongoDB Lookup step.

Getting ready

To get ready for this recipe, you will again need to start your ETL development environment Spoon. Make sure you have the MongoDB server running with the data from the previous chapters and the **Ivy PDI MongoDB Steps** plugin installed in the previous recipe.

How to do it...

Perform the following steps to use MongoDB Lookup:

1. In Spoon, create a new transformation with the name `mongodb-lookup.ktr`.

2. Select the **Design** tab in the left-hand-side view.

3. From the **Input** category folder, find the **Generate Rows** step, and drag and drop it into the working area in the right-hand-side view.

4. Double-click on the step to open the **Generate Rows** dialog.

5. Set **Step Name** to **Get Customer Name**.

6. Next, set the **Limit** field to 1.

7. Add to the **Fields** table the name field as a **String** type with the value as **Euro+ Shopping Channel**.

8. From the **Big Data** category folder, find the **MongoDB Lookup** step, and drag and drop it into the working area in the right-hand-side view.

9. Connect the **Get Customer Name** step to the **MongoDB Lookup** step.

10. Double-click on the step to open the **MongoDB Lookup** configuration dialog.

11. Set **Step Name** to **Get Customer Order Details**.

12. In the **Configure connection** tab, click on the **Get DBs** button and select the SteelWheels option for the **Database** field. Then, click on the **Get collections** button and select the Orders option for the **Collection** field.

13. In the **Fields** tab, click on the **Get fields** button. You should get something like `name = name` by default. However, the collection name field is wrong; set it to `customer.name`.

14. Click on the **Get lookup fields** button to get some of the possible fields available for the documents. Let's keep just the **line, country, postalCode, priceEach, customerNumber, totalPrice,** and **orderLineNumber** fields and remove the others, as you can see in this screenshot:

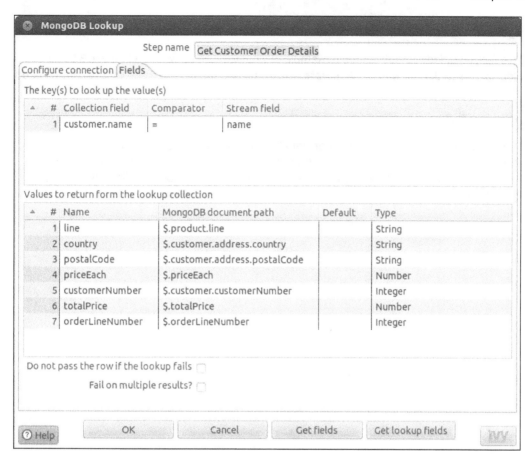

15. From the **Flow** category folder, find the **Dummy (do nothing)** step, and drag and drop it into the working area in the right-hand-side view.

16. Connect the **Get Customer Order Details** step to the **Dummy (do nothing)** step.

17. Double-click on the step to open the **Dummy (do nothing)** configuration dialog.

18. Set **Step Name** to **OUT**.

19. Click on the **OK** button. The transformation should be similar to what is shown in the following screenshot, and you may be able to preview the execution transformation and see the results:

How it works...

This recipe guided you with a simple example of what you can do with the MongoDB Lookup step. We created a row with the **Generate Rows** step and then made the additional data related.

There's more...

The MongoDB Lookup step is an important step for getting additional data into the stream. A good exercise, if you understand this functionality, is to select customers' names from a hypersonic database and making lookups to MongoDB to bring some additional data into the stream.

Index

Thank you for buying
Pentaho Analytics for MongoDB Cookbook

About Packt Publishing

Packt, pronounced 'packed', published its first book, *Mastering phpMyAdmin for Effective MySQL Management*, in April 2004, and subsequently continued to specialize in publishing highly focused books on specific technologies and solutions.

Our books and publications share the experiences of your fellow IT professionals in adapting and customizing today's systems, applications, and frameworks. Our solution-based books give you the knowledge and power to customize the software and technologies you're using to get the job done. Packt books are more specific and less general than the IT books you have seen in the past. Our unique business model allows us to bring you more focused information, giving you more of what you need to know, and less of what you don't.

Packt is a modern yet unique publishing company that focuses on producing quality, cutting-edge books for communities of developers, administrators, and newbies alike. For more information, please visit our website at www.packtpub.com.

About Packt Open Source

In 2010, Packt launched two new brands, Packt Open Source and Packt Enterprise, in order to continue its focus on specialization. This book is part of the Packt open source brand, home to books published on software built around open source licenses, and offering information to anybody from advanced developers to budding web designers. The Open Source brand also runs Packt's open source Royalty Scheme, by which Packt gives a royalty to each open source project about whose software a book is sold.

Writing for Packt

We welcome all inquiries from people who are interested in authoring. Book proposals should be sent to author@packtpub.com. If your book idea is still at an early stage and you would like to discuss it first before writing a formal book proposal, then please contact us; one of our commissioning editors will get in touch with you.

We're not just looking for published authors; if you have strong technical skills but no writing experience, our experienced editors can help you develop a writing career, or simply get some additional reward for your expertise.

PHP and MongoDB Web Development Beginner's Guide

ISBN: 978-1-84951-362-3   Paperback: 292 pages

Combine the power of PHP and MongoDB to build dynamic web 2.0 applications

1. Learn to build PHP-powered dynamic web applications using MongoDB as the data backend.

2. Handle user sessions, store real-time site analytics, build location-aware web apps, and much more, all using MongoDB and PHP.

3. Full of step-by-step instructions and practical examples, along with challenges to test and improve your knowledge.

Pentaho Business Analytics Cookbook

ISBN: 978-1-78328-935-6   Paperback: 392 pages

Over 100 recipes to get you fully acquainted with the key features of Pentaho BA 5 and increase your productivity

1. Gain insight into developing reports, cubes, and data visualizations quickly with Pentaho.

2. Provides an overview of Pentaho's mobile features.

3. Improve your knowledge of Pentaho User Console including tips on how to extend and customize it.

Please check **www.PacktPub.com** for information on our titles